PHOTO ON PRECEDING PAGE BY DAVID GAHR

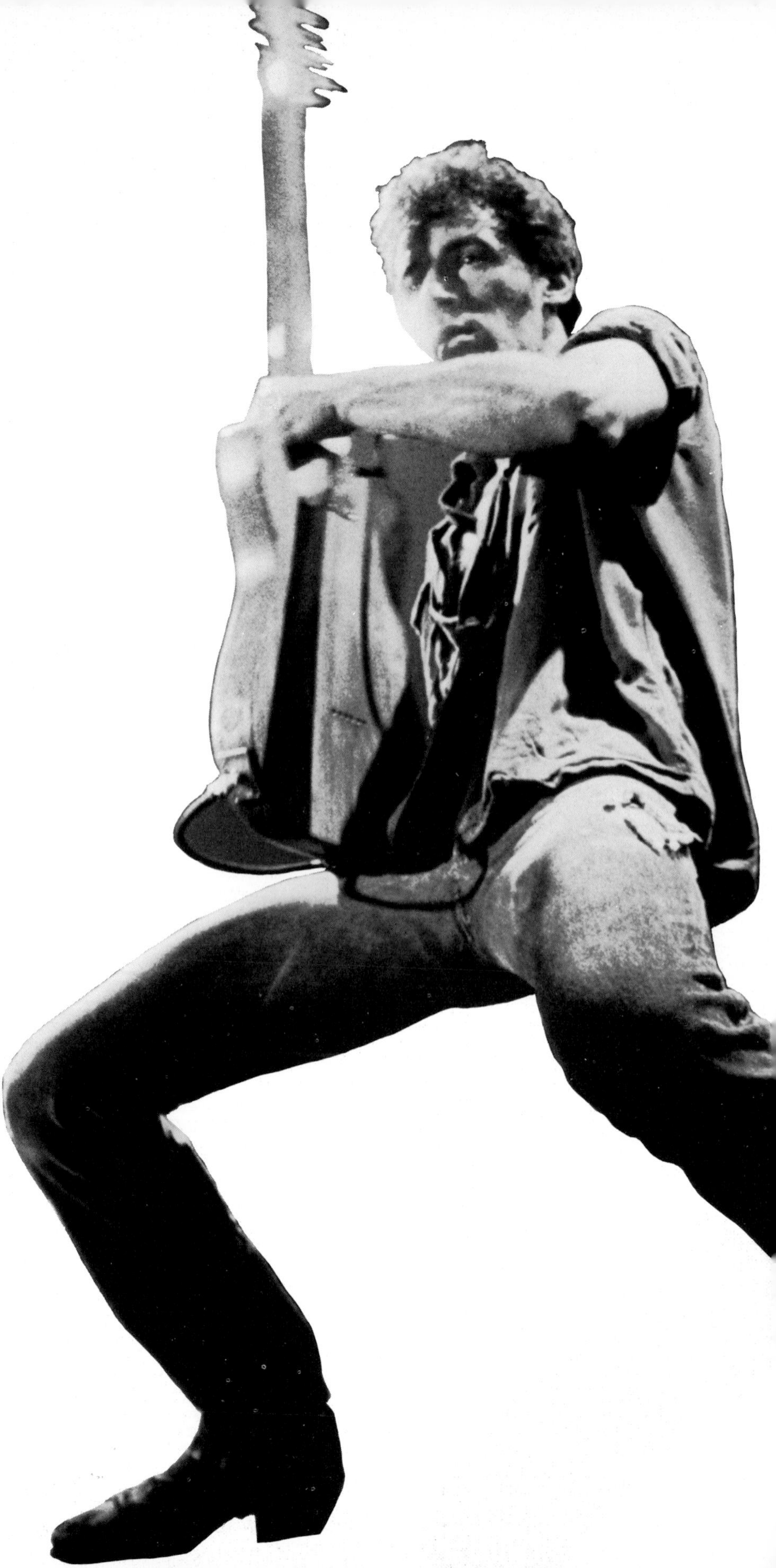

RICHARD McCAFFREE

BRUCE SPRINGSTEEN

Peter Gambaccini

Omnibus Press
London/New York/Sydney/Cologne

This edition published 1985 by Omnibus Press
(A Division of Book Sales Limited)

Published simultaneously in Canada by Central Publishing Co.,
Limited, Toronto.

Designed by Barbara Hoffman.
Cover photograph by Ibet Roberts.

ISBN 0.7119.0696.3
Order No. OP 43397

Executive distributors:
Book Sales Limited
8/9 Frith Street, London W1V 5TZ, England

Music Sales Pty Limited,
120 Rothschild Avenue, Rosebery, NSW 2018,
Australia

To the Music Trade only:
Music Sales Limited
8/9 Frith Street, London W1V 5TZ, England

Printed in England by Dotesios Printers Limited, Trowbridge, Wiltshire

KEN REGAN / CAMERA 5

It takes about seventy-five minutes to drive the fifty miles from Manhattan to Asbury Park, a formerly budding resort town of which its most celebrated man of words and music once said: "If you didn't have enough gas to make it to Atlantic City, you stopped in Asbury."

The citizens of Asbury Park, many of whom live in pleasant Cape Cod -style homes of individual design on small lots, rely heavily on the hotel business and the tourists who ramble along the beaches and the boardwalk in the summer. With local hostelries having names like *Montego Bay Hotel*, the hometown folks might be trying to convince you that you've stumbled into some exotic oasis.

In fact, Asbury Park resembles nothing more than Coney Island fallen on hard times. Its major drawing card today may be that it is one of the few places where you can still play pinball for five cents a game. This is not the vacation spot it once was. Now half black and half white, Asbury Park was the scene of serious race rioting in the early '70s. During the winter, the shops, casinos, and other attractions along the boardwalk are open only on weekends if they are open at all; on a Tuesday or a Wednesday, the place seems to have been evacuated.

Now with gambling casinos attracting millions of would-be Mr. Luckys to Atlantic City, the moneyed traveler has little reason to pay attention to this town.

From this environment has emerged what Los Angeles critic Robert Hilburn has called "the purest glimpse of

7

> *Springsteen is the man who made the much maligned Garden State of New Jersey somehow glamorous and himself famous in the process.*

the passion and pure power of rock 'n' roll in nearly a decade." He is Bruce Springsteen, who has stepped up from his meager beginnings in New Jersey to a level of achievement and esteem that has earned him fan mail from as far away as Finland. Yet it was a form of provinciality that won Springsteen the high status he now enjoys in the music industry. It is by immortalizing the tempestuous, fast and rough life on these boardwalks and streets that he has become such a uniquely respected songwriter and musician. As one writed noted of Springsteen, "green grass, country air, and wide open spaces just aren't Bruce's scene."

Bruce Springsteen was born September 23, 1949 in Freehold, New Jersey, actually a few miles from the shore and Asbury Park, where most of his famed adolescent exploits would occur, and where his family would later reside for several years. Freehold is inland and middle class and undistinguished, hardly the stuff of legend. An album called *Greetings from Freehold, N.J.* might likely have been a complete stiff.

Springsteen is the man who made the much maligned Garden State of New Jersey somehow glamorous and himself famous in the process. He is every bit as marvelous and gifted as his most zealous fans declare, but perhaps most important, he has cut a niche for himself as a rock performer who celebrates the people who were and still are his peers. He would have us believe that he is no more, or less, than the average bloke trying to find a good time on the Asbury Park boardwalk on a Friday or Saturday night.

Bruce's egalitarian image is no accident; unlike many major rock performers, he would never feel disdain for a member of his audience. "I will never put someone in the position of being humiliated," he has said. "It happened to me for too long."

Indeed, if Springsteen's material is so often about being on the move, about getting away from something, it's because the situations in which he found himself in his early years were, almost without exception, miserable.

"I was like nowhere, on the outs," Bruce remembered in a *Crawdaddy* interview. I

had no choice, that's where I was, that's where I got put, that was my place in life all the years I was growing up. I did a lot of running away. And a lot of being brought back. It was always . . . very terrible. It started when I was in the sixth grade."

School days were not good old days for young Bruce. "I hated school. I had the big hate. I remember one time, I was in eighth grade and I wised off and they sent me down to the first grade class and made me sit in these little desks, you know, little chairs. And the sister, she said, 'Show this young man what we do to people who smile in this classroom'—I was probably laughing at being sent down there. And this kid, this six-year-old who has no doubt been taught to do this, he comes over to me—him standing up and me sitting in this little desk are about eye-to-eye—and he slams me in the face. I can feel the sting. I was in shock."

In Catholic school, it seemed Bruce could do no right; when he was uppity to gain the respect of his peers, all he gained was a reputation as "the crazy guy in the class." To punish him, the nuns would

8

take him out of class and keep
him in the adjacent convent
until his parents came to re-
trieve him. "There's this
smell of religion, this smell
that convents have, well, every
time I went there I got sick, I
just threw up."

Despite his surname, Bruce
is mostly Italian; his Grand-
father Zirilli is credited as the
source of his ability to spin
yarns, many of them about
the excruciating pains of his
young years.

"In the third grade a nun
stuffed me into a garbage can
she kept under her desk because she told me that's where
I belonged," he said in *Newsweek*. "I also had the distinction of being the only altar
boy knocked down by a priest
on the steps of the altar during Mass. The old priest got
mad. My mom wanted me to
learn how to serve Mass but I
didn't know what I was doin'
so I was tryin' to fake it."

The youngster in New Jer-
sey became an outsider living
a very solitary existence. "I
didn't even make it to class
clown, I had nowhere near
that amount of notoriety. I
didn't have, like, the flair to
be the complete jerk. It was
like I didn't exist; it was the
wall, then me."

He remembers, "I lived
half of my first thirteen years
in a trance or something.
People thought I was weird
because I always went around
with this *look* on my face. I
was thinking of things, but I
was always on the outside,
looking in."

By his senior year in high
school he and his fellow stu-
dents mutually ignored each
other. He almost didn t graduate "because the kids in my
class wouldn't let me. I was

playing in bands and my hair was real long and the sister got up in front of everybody and said 'Class, don't you have any pride in yourselves? Are you going to allow this boy to embarrass you and go to graduation looking like that?' And they weren't gonna let me graduate unless I cut my hair."

On graduation day, Bruce "left the house and didn't come back." He left for New York to stay with a friend. His parents reached him there; his mother called and said there was a graduation party at his house. As he recalled in *Crawdaddy*, Bruce appeared at the front door with a girl, and his father "pulls me inside by the collar with one hand, leaves her outside—I don't see her again for a while—drags me up to my room, and *takes out all the light bulbs* so I've got to sit there in the dark by myself"

To a concert audience, with his parents among the thousands in attendance, Bruce would say "when I was growing up there were two things that were unpopular in my house: one was me, the other was my guitar."

Bruce could evoke a morbid kind of humor even from the most painful memories, as when he'd explain how his father didn't know what kind of guitar he was playing—Gibson, Fender, or whatever. "I always remember him sticking his head in the door and saying, 'Turn down that *goddamn* guitar.' He must've thought that all that stuff in my room was the same make, 'cause it used to be 'Turn down that *goddamn* radio,' and 'Get that *goddam* record off that *goddam* stereo.' God was damning a lot of stuff in

RICHARD McCAFFREE

my room."

When Bruce was growing up his family moved frequently; "I lived in practically every single town around here, from Atlantic Highlands to Bradley Beach." Many of the grammar school years were spent in a house on Institute Street in Asbury Park, in close proximity to a Nestle's factory.

"When it rained," Bruce remembers, we smelled that stuff all day long."

In those days Bruce's father Douglas Springsteen never made more than $10,000 a year, at jobs at the Nestle's factory as a gardener, or as a prison guard. For much of Bruce's childhood, his family (including two younger sisters) lived with his grandparents.

Bruce recalls that his father "was a driver. He liked to get in the car and just drive. He got everybody else in the car too and he made *us* drive. He made us all drive." If Bruce's own lyrics and legend are to be believed, driving is one passion of his father's that he kept.

"I figured out we were

pretty much alike," Springsteen said of his father in the *Time* cover story. "My father never has much to say to me, but I know he thinks about a lot of things. I know he's driving himself crazy thinking about these things . . . and yet he sure ain't got much to say when we sit down to talk." His father is now a bus driver in San Mateo, California.

Bruce hasn't had a lot to say for publication about his mother Adele, who worked as a secretary when he was young, but in *Time* he said she was "just like Superwoman, she did everything, everywhere, all the time."

A tormented kid like Bruce needed some outlet, a bit of a promise of escape from his dreary existence Originally, he wanted to play the drums but couldn't afford a set.

A guitar was cheaper. And after seeing Elvis Presley on "The Ed Sullivan Show," nine-year-old Bruce couldn't imagine anyone not wanting to be like Elvis. The next day he picked up a guitar "and then I quickly put it down when I found I couldn't play it."

But he was convinced of what he wanted to do, and he had a model. "That Elvis, man, he is all there is," Springsteen observed later. "There ain't no more. Everything starts and ends with him. He wrote the book. He is everything to do and not to do in the business."

The unhappy child had his own personal visions of redemption and resurrection. Once, when asked by a nun to draw a picture of Jesus, Bruce sketched a picture of Christ crucified on a guitar.

Being an unpopular teenager forced Bruce to seek an

RICHARD McCAFFREE

interest of his own, something he could do by himself. For him, it was music. "A lot of rock 'n' roll people, that's where they came from, just this solitary existence," he has observed. "If you're gonna be good at something, you gotta be alone a lot to practice, there has to be a certain involuntariness to it."

Springsteen is not the only rock star to observe this truism. Leslie West, the gargantuan guitarist for *Mountain,* was severely ostracized for being an overweight teenager. While other youngsters were out playing baseball or football, West was at home in his room, playing his guitar for hours and hours.

Out of the solitary anguish of Van Gogh's French village, Proust's corklined room, or Bruce Springsteen's small New Jersey home, important and outstanding art can be hatched.

The self-esteem that music provided to young Springsteen is immeasurable. "Rock 'n' roll has been everything to me," he said in *Newsweek.* "The first day I can remember lookin' in the mirror and standin' what I was seein' was the day I had a guitar in my hand."

"Music saved me," Bruce would later state. "From the beginning, my guitar was something I could go to. If I hadn't found music, I don't know what I would have done."

Finding music wasn't an instantaneous panacea for Springsteen. He was still far from a BMOC, still awkward socially.

Bruce fondly recalls his gruesome school dances, gut wrenching as the experience was at the time.

"I've been staring this girl down for hours and I don't aim my sights too high, if you know what I mean," he begins explaining. "It's five to ten, five to eleven, whenever the dances used to end, and a song like this (a slow dance tune) would come on. So I start walking across the dance floor, and let me tell you, that is a *long* walk. Many a night I never made it across.

"Y'know, I'd start walking and get halfway, then turn back. 'Cause you weren't asking a girl, 'Do you want to dance?' You were asking her, 'Do you WANTA? My life is in your hands!' We're not talking about a dance; we're talking about SURVIVAL. If she said no . . . But if she said yes, you were *saved*."

Being a bit of a social pariah wounded the sensitive youngster. A strict Catholic education was a source of sorrow as well.

"I was raised Catholic and everybody who was raised Catholic hates religion. They hate it, they can't stand it," Springsteen told *Creem* writer Robert Duncan. Springsteen want to Catholic school and church every Sunday as a boy.

'I quit that stuff when I was in eighth grade. By the time you're older than thirteen it's too ludicrous to go along with anymore. By the time I was in eighth grade I just lost it all. I decided to go to public high school, and that was a big deal.

"If you got up in eighth grade and said that next year you were going to Freehold Regional it was like . . . 'Are you *insane*??? You are dirt! You are the worst! You're a . . . *barbarian!*' "

Most of Bruce's public statements about his Catholic upbringing and education, and the lyrics of some of his later songs, indicate that the experience was one of anguish and torture. But he could kid about it. A 1975 colloquy with Al Rudis in the *Chicago Sun-Times* demonstrated how Bruce could sometimes put on reporters:

Q: You were raised a Catholic and went to church schools. Do you still go to church?

A: Every Sunday.

Q: Would you say you re a good Catholic?

A: Yeah.

Q: What about some of the lines in your songs that sound anti-Church, for instance the one in "Lost in the Flood," about pregnant nuns running through the Vatican pleading immaculate conception?

A: I wrote that a long time ago.

Q: Then did you have a falling out with religion and then go back?

A: No, man, I don't go to church. (Here there is a hearty laugh, as if to indicate that his earlier answers about being religious were put-ons). I ain't been to church in eight years. I don't believe in any of that stuff.

A more somber Bruce observes "I don't remember anything nice about it, so I guess I didn't enjoy it. I never talk about it. It has nothing to do with me. I'm not involved in it." His conclusion? "Some people pray, some people play music."

13

Bruce saved eighteen dollars to buy his first guitar, which he remembers as "one of the most beautiful sights I have ever seen in my life." In his early performing days, there were some strange avenues for rock music. "We used to play the Elks Club, the Rollerdome, and the local insane asylum," he recalled. "We were always terrified at the asylum. One time this guy in a suit got up and introduced us for twenty minutes sayin' we were greater than the Beatles. Then the doctors came up and took him away."

The early gigs were also held at places like Sing Sing prison, trailer parks, a Shop-Rite parking lot, and a drive-in, where Bruce's band played under the screen at intermission. At a place like the Upstage in Asbury Park, they'd play from 8 p.m. to 5 a.m. and make fifteen dollars.

Bruce was making the trip to play in small New York clubs at sixteen. He was given one valuable lesson: "I learned earlier than most people you had to write your own material."

In 1968, Bruce was playing in Greenwich Village at places like the Cafe Wha and the Night Owl, occasionally performing with Circus Maximus, Jerry Jeff Walker's old group. Their big hit was "The Wind."

Back in Jersey, Bruce and his band buddies had a few extra matters to contend with. In *Playboy*, Springsteen told Richard Price, "this club owner contacted me and said if I didn't show up at his place on Saturday night with a band, he'd kill me (for economic reasons, Bruce was solo at the time)."

"Now, I played family clubs in New Jersey that were pretty rough, but this guy was serious. He knew where I lived. Yeah. Some of those club owners were crazy. There was one guy, pulled out a gun one night and shot an amplifier. Can you see it? Smoke curling up to the ceiling. Absolutely quiet. And he says, 'I told you guys to turn down.' "

Bruce's bands changed names and lineups with great frequency in his teens and early twenties. Steel Mill, his

group in his late teens, was "a Humble Pie-type band," and photos indicate that he had shoulder-length hair in those days.

A later alliance, Dr. Zoom and the Sonic Boom, sounds like it may have been a bit like Captain Beefheart and the Magic Band; apparently, knowledge of a musical instrument wasn't a requirement for being in the group. "Somebody'd take a solo and we'd all fall down laughing," Bruce remembers of that outfit. Among other things, he was joined on stage by a Monopoly board, for reasons known only to himself.

Springsteen used his own name to front a later ten-piece group, which little by little shrunk to five for monetary purposes. The nucleus of this incarnation included Danny Federici and Vini Lopez, who would both be on Springsteen's first album, *Greetings from Asbury Park, N.J.*

By the start of the '70s, Bruce and his cronies had enough of a local following to "draw two, maybe three thousand people on any given night." But those were not milk and honey days, as Bruce told *The Aquarian* in a visit back to his old Asbury Park haunts.

"Nobody would book us because we never did any Top 40. *Never.* We used to play all old soul stuff. Chuck Berry, just the things we liked. That's why we couldn't get booked. We made enough to eat though."

After awhile, however, the fun faded even further. "The kicks started to wear off and a lot of the time we didn't make enough to eat. That's why I signed with Mike [Appel] Anything was better than what was happening at the time."

For a great part of these scuffling days, Bruce was living upstairs over a surfboard factory owned by Carl "Tinker" West. He even tried his hand at surfing.

"Since I was from Freehold, I was considered inland," he told an *Aquarian* writer in a visit to his old haunts in 1978. "All these guys used to surf everyday. I was friends with'em all but never went. Finally, they got to me. One afternoon they were merciless. They just kept taunting me and kidding me about not surfing that it just sorta got me riled. I grabbed a board and we all headed out to the beach.

"I must have been some sight surfing for the first time," recalls Bruce "but I'll tell you something—I got the hang of it pretty quick. Hell, it ain't harder than anything else. It's like riding a bike. I haven't surfed in awhile. Now that's something I'd love to do. As a matter of fact, I think I will."

Tinker West was an important man in Bruce's life. He was his benefactor and even his manager, and it was Tinker who taught Bruce how to drive at the fairly advanced age of nineteen. Without that expertise it's conceivable that half or more of the inspiration for Springsteen's material would be missing.

It was Tinker who introduced Springsteen to Mike Appel. Appel, whose previous claim to fame was his coauthorship of a Partridge Family hit called "Doesn't Somebody Want to Be Wanted," immediately saw the burgeoning talent in Bruce and encouraged him to keep writing new

material. When Appel would call Springsteen to a meeting in New York Bruce would come in by bus from New Jersey and write a song while in transit.

The large minded Appel was to compare Bruce to, among others, Dylan, Shakespeare, Wordsworth, Byron, and Keats. He publicly professed a desire to be "the next Albert Grossman," and even went so far as to rent out offices once occupied by Grossman, Bob Dylan's former manager.

Appel believed Bruce was just what the public wanted. "The industry is at the bottom of the barrel," he said in *Newsweek* in 1975. "We've got people scratching around looking for new talent. There's an amazing paucity of talent because there hasn't been anyone isolated enough to create a distinctive point of view. What I'm waiting for, what Bruce Springsteen is waiting for, and we're all waiting for is something that makes you want to dance!"

John Hammond was to call Appel "as offensive as any man I've ever met, but he's utterly selfless in his devotion to Bruce." It was Hammond whom Appel called at Columbia with news of his prodigiously talented client.

On a fateful day Hammond's secretary told him "I think you might do this. He came on very strong." She was referring to a call from Mike Appel.

Hammond, Columbia Records Vice President of Talent Acquisition, was responsible for a long list of artists from Billie Holiday to Bob Dylan. Acknowledging Hammond's discovery of Dylan, Appel reportedly told him "we wanna

see if that was just a fluke, or if you really have ears."
Moxie has its merits; Hammond yelled "Stop, you're making me hate you," but a meeting was arranged in his office, where Bruce would sing and play guitar unaccompanied.

"I'd been reading this book [Anthony Scaduto's biography of Dylan] and read about how it all went down and about John Hammond Sr. and stuff," Bruce reflected. "Then I went in and met Mike and he said he was takin' me in to see Hammond. I didn't get nervous. I figured nothin' would happen. It was amazing to me, reading that book and then I find myself sitting there in that office."

"I went into a state of shock as soon as I walked in," Springsteen told an interviewer later. "Before I ever played a note Mike starts screamin' and yellin' 'bout me. I'm shrivelin' up and thinkin' 'Please, Mike, give me a break. Let me play a damn song.' So, dig this, before I ever played a note the hype began."

The first song Bruce played was "Saint in the City." Within two hours, Hammond had booked him at the Gaslight in New York. Hammond was overwhelmed; Springsteen was signed to the label in twenty-four hours. The record executive was to comment later that he recognized "at once that Bruce would last a generation."

"The kid absolutely knocked me out," Hammond told *Newsweek* of the historic 1972 confrontation. "I only hear somebody really good once every ten years, and not only was Bruce the best, he was a lot

15

better than Dylan when I first heard *him*."

Hammond also detected a Springsteen trait that made his image as a rock star for the people seem all the more real. "In all my years in this business," he said of Bruce, "he is the only person I've met who cares absolutely nothing about money."

Bruce himself verified that impression in a later interview with *Exit* writer David Fandray. "I never did anything for money, when I was a kid, 'cause I seen it kill my old

man," he said. "Money is a cheap way to get easy respect."

Hammond brought the matter of Bruce directly to Columbia President Clive Davis. Davis showed his enthusiasm, but in few words. After he heard a tape of Springsteen, Davis remarked "he's very amusing, isn't he?" When pursued on the matter by *Crawdaddy* editor Peter Knobler, Davis suggested "he's refreshing." Springsteen was said to be quite touched when he received personal Christmas wishes from Davis in Decem-

ber of 1972.

Bruce's first album for Columbia, *Greetings from Asbury Park N.J.*, was completed in September but would not be released until January of 1973.

The brash Appel worked fast. Before *Greetings* was even released, Appel was on the telephone offering the NBC producer of the Super Bowl the services of Springsteen to sing "The Star Spangled Banner."

Appel was informed that NBC had contracted Andy Williams for the anthem and

Blood, Sweat, and Tears for a half-time performance. He reportedly yelled, "they're losers and you're a loser too. Someday I'm going to give you a call and remind you of this, then I'm going to make another call and you'll be out of a job."

Bruce had made his trips into New York to play when he was young and unknown but the first Manhattan gig for Bruce as the Columbia contract player was at Kenny's Castaways, a small Village bistro. *Crawdaddy* was to declare "the only comparable experience could have been if someone had ushered you into Big Pink in 1967 and you'd never heard of Dylan. Two completely different sets a night over an entire weekend, and every song infinitely personal and completely universal. Words which stung with their clarity woke you up fast and were instant intimates. No question, nothing would ever be the same again." The magazine proclaimed "he was instantly the best performer fronting the best performing band in the country."

The man who once ran Max's Kansas City in New York later became a Columbia Records executive. Faris Bouhafa told the Philadelphia publication the *Drummer*, that "the first shows [at Max's] were very spontaneous. Bruce has always done the street raps on stage and he always had an incredible sense of drama. After a while, every moment looked spontaneous, but he'd been doing it so long it had to be calculated."

As 1972 ended, Bruce reflected, in an interview with Peter Knobler, on the difference a year made. "Last winter I wrote like a madman," he observed. "Put it out. Had no money, nowhere to go, nothing to do. Didn t know too many people. It was cold and I wrote a lot. And I got to feeling very guilty if I didn't. Terrible guilt feelings. Like it was masturbation. That bad!"

With the first album due out, at least a measure of success for Springsteen seemed imminent. "People used to tell me that to be a success I should say I was from New York City. Oh yeah, and that I'd better change my name! Even my mother, when I told her I had a recording contract, said 'what'll you call yourself now?' But you are who you are, it's obvious, isn't it? The one thing I learned is to be real."

And he learned it all on the streets and shores of New Jersey. "The summer I was doing the first album and the summer before that I spent a lot of time in Asbury," he would later say of that crucial period. "But all the heavy personal stuff in my songs comes from spending time further up the beach."

Greetings from Asbury Park, N.J. was completed in September 1972 and appeared in January 1973. The timing, in one sense, should have been just about perfect for Bruce to make a commercial splash. Rock was aching for another male minstrel, and electric balladeer for a mass audience. It would be almost a year before Bob Dylan would emerge from a prolonged period of inactivity. Jackson Browne was still a minor figure, having released only one sparse, modest album. Neil Young's career and mood were both in decline; fans weren't prepared to accept his obsession with the darker side of the counterculture, and were deserting in droves.

However, there was a more significant development in the music business that made the climate for an artist like Bruce Springsteen less than cozy in 1973. Music, as all else, is subject to cycles, and Springsteen seemed to have come in on the wrong end of one.

Popular music had been dominated since the beginnings of rock and roll by AM radio and its format of simple, easy to remember songs that were over in three minutes. But the the mid-'60s musicians on both sides of the Atlantic became bored by the limitations of a concern with churning out hits. Lyrical statements became more substan-

18

tial and complex, and instrumentalists burst beyond the shackles of the "song" format. Rock's major virtuosos, first on guitar and later on the keyboard, gained exposure on "progressive" radio stations, and their popularity quickly surpassed that of artists who depended on AM support.

By 1973, that situation seemed to be coming full circle. It once again became important for a performer to have a "hit," something familiar audiences would recognize. The best illustration of this was Rod Stewart. A critical favorite, Stewart had released two solo albums of lyrical eloquence and sensitivity and original and tastefully arranged music. Few people bought either *The Rod Stewart Album* or *Gasoline Alley*.

His next album was *Every Picture Tells A Story,* with a dazzling title song that may be rock's best counterpart to *The Odyssey.* It was not, however, the much hoped for breakthrough to superstar status for Stewart.

That came with "Maggie May," a far more artistically minor track on the same album. "Maggie May" was brief and basic, with words everyone could remember. It became a monstrous hit single for Rod, although it paled beside earlier and greater efforts.

Henceforth, Stewart's emphasis was on loading his albums with surefire hit songs that would get plenty of AM airplay. The progressive FM stations who wanted the latest from Rod ended up playing the same material. A major artist, virtually ignored, had taken the singles route to success. It would not be long

before "hook" became a byword in the record industry. Producers and artists were constantly looking for sounds the public could hook on to and easily assimilate. Soon, record company executives were demanding that even their most established performers not release an album unless it contained at least one probable hit single.

Greetings was hardly the kind of album to fill that bill. On the face of it, no thought at all was given to choosing singles. To his credit, Springsteen made no artistic compromise to simplicity His was an amalgamation of the sounds he'd grown up with, the music he'd heard on the radio and in New Jersey night spots. It was a hybrid of the best of Bruce's background; it was not watered down by a drop.

And *Greetings* was hardly easy to assimilate. Memorizing the lyrics to any of the album's nine compositions would have been a far tougher homework assignment than learning the prologue to *Henry V* or *Hamlet's* soliloquy. It is a task the likes of which eager fans had not been faced with since the days of Dylan's "Subterranean Homesick Blues" and "Bringing It All Back Home."

Greetings from Asbury Park, N.J. is an incredibly ambitious venture, especially for a debut album. Springsteen attempts to do more lyrically with a rock musical format than anyone since and including Dylan. The images he presents for us to absorb come on like a cloud of locusts—rapidly and without warning and by the thousands. And the cast of characters is immense;

one writer counted eighty-six different personages on the album.

No one could listen to Bruce sprint through "Blinded by the Light" and seize and envision every picture he paints for us. We'd appreciate the assistance of some sort of stop action camera, so we could do a freeze frame on each line of Springsteen's decidely uncommon verse.

The album is packaged as a picture postcard, a not inappropriate conceit for a journey through one of the postcard capitals of America, with its steel piers, boardwalk, casinos, and salt water.

There's a lot more to this trip than postcard imagery, however, and our tour guide is commemorated properly on a postage stamp on the backside. He's kind of scruffy and gaunt and young (only 24, mind you,) for an authoritative source on "an ocean resort in east central New Jersey" (*Webster s New World Dictionary*). Yet there is aged wisdom in the eyes, and something knowing in the smile.

"Blinded by the Light" is verbose, some detractors have said, and there is truth to that. It is also, in spots, obscure It's admittedly difficult to absorb, and it would be easy just to walk away at the outset and say 'what does this mean'?

But the same could be said of the paintings of Hieronymus Bosch and Pieter Breughel. Both men loaded their canvases chockful of perhaps a few too many scenes in a single frame, and not all of what they showed us could be comprehended.

So listen. This is the first

19

song on the first side of the first Bruce Springsteen record; this is our introduction to Bruce and his world, where he struggled, where he hung out and did his thinking when he was broke, unknown, unheralded.

Bruce, playing all the guitars on *Greetings,* and Clarence Clemons on sax propel the song from the beginning as the Springsteen couplets begin to zing at us. The cast of characters commences with the now familiar "Madman drummers, bummers, and Indians in the summer, with a teenage diplomat."

Springsteen's uncommon rhyming scheme helps give the song its perfect symmetry. Each phrase contains three rhyming words and a fourth that rhymes with the end of the subsequent phrase.

They don't teach that in English lit. That's a difficult form to maintain, but Springsteen is not one to take the easy way out. Nor does he do anything on a small scale. While we may be used to guys with chips on their shoulders, Bruce walks up to us "with a boulder on my shoulder, feelin' kinda older."

"Blinded," with its twenty syllables per line, serves its purpose as an album opener, awakening us to the panorama of Springsteen's Asbury Park. The people here are types that will populate so many of his songs. A stroll down the boardwalk reveals people who seem stuck, in tough situations or tough relationships some of which can be understood only by the author. Yet the song seems oddly optimistic. As soon as we hear of their woes, we get Bruce's assurances that they'll be okay. Everybody's "gonna make it tonight." Even the guy with the worst of troubles. "I unsnapped his skullcap and in between his ears I saw a gap but figured he'd be all right," notes the comforting Bruce. The final line is Bruce in a nutshell. He doesn't flinch from anything. "Mama always told me not to look into the sights of the sun/Oh but mama, that's where the fun is."

There have been many attempts to define the sound of early Bruce Springsteen, as heard in "Blinded by the Light." The most appropriate could be "Bob Dylan with Van Morrison's backup band." The light sax and organ backing gives Bruce's early music the same kind of free flowing jazz feel found in much of Morrison's repertoire. And the importance of Clarence Clemons to the Springsteen sound is manifested here in his very first recorded track.

Saxophone had been the important virtuosos' instrumentation of '50s and early '60s music; in the first decade of rock and roll you will probably discover twice as many sax solos as piano or guitar breaks. That is the music Springsteen was raised on, the sound he honed in his fledgling local bands in his adolescent years.

Indeed, on the basis of *Greetings from Asbury Park, N.J.,* we can only assume that Bruce's immersion in the music from the mid-'60s to today was quite selective, or that much of it passed through his consciousness without leaving a trace of influence.

Dylan and Van Morrison quite obviously left an impression, and the lyrical ambitiousness of the period is matched and surpassed by Bruce. Beyond that, it would appear that New Jersey was a kind of time and space warp for the maturing Springsteen. There is nothing of *Greetings,* or on any of the later albums for that matter, to suggest

that Bruce had even heard West Coast psychedelia as represented by the Jefferson Airplane and Grateful Dead, nor of its perhaps too logical by-product and successor, the "laid back" sound of The Eagles and Jackson Browne.

When *Greetings from Asbury Park, N.J.* was released, the most influential popular musician in the English-speaking world, in terms of the audible and occasionally visible effect he had on other performers, was David Bowie, direct from his success as Ziggy Stardust. Bruce and Bowie were like oil and water; there is virtually nothing that the two have in common.

This is significant because by 1975, on the strength of "Born to Run," Springsteen was to eclipse Bowie completely as rock's most imitated and emulated performer. Today, Bruce has an even stronger hold on that distinction.

Asbury Park is hardly a gigantic metropolis, but it is a bustling, bristling, teeming center as interpretated by Springsteen. There's a whole lot of action going on, the kind of action one associates with the city, not rural Vermont. Springsteen, as would be seen to an even greater extent later on, was once again making rock the sound of the city. Giving a prominent role to the saxophone was extremely crucial to an urban sound, Springsteen understood. Not surprisingly the sax would be the most striking element of Gerry Rafferty's "Baker Street," the outstanding "urban" single of the '70s.

Dylan, of course was urban-based in his most creative period. He had borrowed from and contributed to the legend that the area loosely defined as Greenwich Village was the place where the important ideas were being hatched where the vital art was being created, where one could be enlightened by just breathing the air and absorbing the environment.

Both Dylan and Springsteen are perspicacious, a two-dollar word meaning they understand what they see. But they chose to see things differently. Dylan preferred to observe; Springsteen almost always opted for action. These may be two of rock's most important urban poets, but one tended to the introspective, while the other was marvelously and unabashedly exuberant.

The Springsteen of *Greetings from Asbury Park, N.J.* is young, energetic, and makes few apologies. In a world of rock that was beginning to emphasize the jaded, the decadent, or the far too mellow, here was a positive dynamo. 33 1/3 could hardly contain this boy.

Plenty of people who were Bruce's peers in age had tired of rock, with its severe excesses and failed potential, but fortunately Bruce hadn't stopped playing what they yearned to hear.

Excited folks whose new obsessions were jazz, theatre, or even their own jobs were reawakening a ritual that they thought had died forever. Excited Bruce buffs were inviting friends over to hear this guy who was not stale, not bland. The suspicious retained their doubts, until the opening strains of "Blinded by the Light." Here was a guy who was saying something, and saying it with enthusiasm.

The appeal of Bruce to the lapsed rock audience that was now in its middle or late twenties is almost without parallel. This was the age group that started most of the country's major music publications during the progressive era of the late '60s, and many of the same people continued to run the magazines even as their interest in rock dwindled and the focus of the magazines and their readers moved beyond music to encompass other concerns. The critical praises that were quickly heaped on Bruce were largely messages of thanks from writers who were weary of covering glitter rock, teeny bopper rock, and other unfortunate trends of the times.

If a large segment of the rock listening population had drifted away (of course, to be replaced by even younger partisans), it would logically be because they believed rock music no longer served the purpose it had a few years before. It had once been their pulse and their voice, but it had drifted from its middle to unredeeming "heavy metal" on the one end and totally lifeless blandness on the other.

Idols had been proven fallible. From Woodstock emerged Woodstock Nation, a name and concept first coined by Abbie Hoffman. Rock was this nation's unifying force and its musicians were its prophets. Music was the foundation of an idyllic, Utopian new culture. Rock, it seemed, could save the world.

Such thinking, though naive, was reasonably preva-

lent, and any number of artists were willing to wear the messianic mantles thrust upon them. No one, of course, was equal to the task. The nation of rock was a good thing, and all good things get bilked commercially. It turned sour and it turned ugly. It didn't take long to realize once again that they were dealing with a mortal universe, and that these gods they'd created were mere men and women.

Naive true believers fall hard when their innocence is betrayed. The subsequent cynicism can be even crueler than its root cause. The posturings of onetime idols, formerly taken as gospel, now were seen as hollow, insincere, and dated.

The causes of disillusionment were many. Politics are not unconnected with the trend. Years of feverish radical activity, often at great risk to one's education, career, and even life, had apparently yielded nothing in 1973. The war did not end; the McCarthy and McGovern crusades were horrendous failures, and both men appeared stained and lessened by their defeats.

Unselfish collectivism had failed; the wounded survivors scattered and did not regroup. The era of the individual arose, with a president who was out to market himself at all costs as its precursor.

Many Woodstock nationals found no difficulty in dedicating themselves to the pursuit of their own interests in what came to be known as the "me decade." Others, who still held on to shreds of belief that there could be a greater good based on more than the

25

TOM HILL

glorification of the self, had no focal point any longer. Rock became big business. It probably always had been, but much of America was only awakening to it.

Thus as 1973 began, the children of the '60s were looking for something to latch on to, something to get excited about. It wouldn't be anyone with the social and political pretentions of the artists of the '60s. Indeed, "pretentious" became a heinous label, second only to "murderer." For many of the dissillusioned, there would be no more blind faith; everything was suspect; everyone had to prove overwhelmingly that he should be trusted and heeded.

Yet there was still plenty of energy there, both physical and intellectual, yearning for a fresh new outlet. The man of the '80s was here in the flesh and on vinyl in 1973, but the normal channels that would carry his message to the masses had deteriorated so badly that only limited numbers would know about him until 1975.

Something better was what these folks wanted, and Springsteen was here to offer it. Music was still their language, the art form that they best understood and the one that had grown out of their youthful fervor. For awhile, lost amidst the drivel that flooded the airways and the album charts, the fervor had no outlet.

"Growin' Up" picks up where "Blinded" left off, with a few piano ticklings by Dave Sancious as a launching pad for an allegory about Bruce's Asbury Park adolescence. It helps to know a bit

about what kind of teenager Bruce was to appreciate this song, to know that those clever-sounding phrases actually have a ring of truth.

We can imagine, for example, that Bruce frequently "combed my hair till it was just right and commanded the night brigade;" if we learn that Bruce was a loner often cruelly ostracized by his classmates, and that he was not reluctant to do battle with teachers, we understand "I strolled all alone through a fallout zone and came out with my soul untouched/ I

hid in the clouded wrath of the crowd but when they said 'sit down' I stood up." And when we find out that he used to walk around deep in thought with a weird dazed look on his face, "I took month-long vacations in the stratosphere and you know it's really hard to hold your breath" makes sense.

"Growin' Up" moves at a brisk clip, propelled mainly by Sancious, the most frequently heard instrumentalist on this album. The song starts and ends with him, as if he were picked up in progress and was, at the end, deserted in the middle of something to be rejoined later. Sancious is the connective tissue on side one of *Greetings,* the man who makes it all seem like a suite.

It is all a suite, with one gruesome exception—"Mary Queen of Arkansas," a real mistake and probably the worst song Springsteen has ever put to plastic. Bruce solos on guitar and harmonica and although the sound of the harmonica muted in the distance is appropriately eerie, nothing else about this song is admirable, beginning with the reference to Mary's body as a "soft hulk." Since neither the music nor the words are strong enough to convey any sense of urgency, Bruce tries too hard to do so with his voice. The results are actually painful and tough to listen to.

One would hope this isn't any indication of what would have resulted if *Greetings* had been entirely an acoustic solo album as had originally been planned. Maybe the guys in the band just knew better and elected to sit this one out. We're back to the real busi-

ness at hand as we pick up Sancious again for just a few notes that lead into "Does This Bus Stop at 82nd Street?" One thing Bruce made sure of on *Greetings* is that he equipped his songs with strong opening lines, the kind that make you take notice and anxious to hear what follows. The beginning seems like truly generous advice: "Hey bus driver keep the change, bless your children, give them names/ Don't trust men who walk with canes/ Drink this and you'll grow wings on your feet."

The music is lively and chipper; this could be Bruce, somehow wide awake in the morning or whenever he gets up, popping onto the bus and watching as the panorama of Broadway sweeps by; there's no plot just hoardes of Springsteen images of "wizard imps and sweat sock pimps, interstellar nymphs" and sundry other personae.

Everybody's got their own favorite among the lines that dash by—"tainted women in Vistavision perform for out-of-state kids at the late show" is marvelously evocative. But the one that sticks in the cranium is the message that the mere presence of Bruce delivers to many of his fans; when the Daily News asks Mary Lou for the dope, she says "Man, the dope's that there's still hope."

Actually, the hope here quickly dissipates as 'Does This Bus Stop at 82nd Street?" gives way to "Lost in the Flood," its harrowing alter ego. Springsteen is a spectator at what seems like an urban Armageddon, with a cast of forlorn characters drowning in quicksand, blood oil, or the

27

omnipresent flood. It's a chaotic nightmare in which "nuns run bald through Vatican halls, pleading immaculate conception/ And everybody's wrecked on Main Street from drinking unholy blood." The jaded survivors can only make comments like "Hey man, did you see that? His body hit the street with such a beautiful thud."

As the grisliness unfolds Bruce becomes more impassioned, Sancious' organ runs circles around the madness, and Springsteen must know "I wonder what they were gettin' into, or were they just lost in the flood?" The question remains unanswered but the impact of the strewn landscape lingers, bringing side one to a dramatic finish.

Side two opens with the decidely slight but still enthralling "The Angel" a short composition sung almost *a cappella*; there is only meager piano, with which Sancious nevertheless creates a sense of mounting tension, and a few final bars of upright bass by guest performer Richard Davis. Davis' deep somber chords have "tragedy" written all over them.

"The Angel" is a somber meditation on the mixed joys of motorcycling, with the character of the title "wieldin' love as a lethal weapon on his way to hubcap heaven." Which is exactly where he ends up; at the end, a young girl, "Madison Avenue's claim to fame in a trainer bra with eyes like rain," is staring at a heap of his broken bones.

Bruce turns in one of his better vocal performances here, subdued at first, a little more anguished as death lies ahead. Most of it's done in

his patented half-singing, half-groaning voice that manages to imbue each lyric with a multitude of meanings, each emotion with a complicated blend of feeling.

One characteristic of Springsteen's compositions on *Greetings* that may have prevented him from achieving overwhelming commercial success the first time out is that their meaning is not always completely accessible. "For You," for example, seems at first hearing to have a few elements conducive to a hit single, as if it could have been the song to sell this album to AM radiophiles.

Musically it presents no problems with its simple piano-based instrumentation and even hummable melody. And he's singing "I came for you, for you" more than a few times. That's great; songs about former suitors returning to claim their lost loves are frequently hit bound.

But hold on! These two folks have one helluva relationship. He expresses a sense of commitment nicely: "To her Cheshire smile I'll stand on file, she's all I ever wanted." But what's with this girl, whose "barroom eyes shine vacancy, to see her you gotta look hard"? There are references to waiting at Bellevue, a Chelsea suicide, taking turns playing God, his finding her broken on the beach, she clinging like a leech, his urgency and her lifelong emergency. Hey folks, this ain't Paul and Paula!

It's an awful lot to swallow, and you'd have to listen 100 times to take it all in You don't have to take it *all* in to enjoy it; it's another lyrical bombardment—we should be

used to it by now—so don't fret about the occasional obscurity. This is another one of those tunes where you seize the images you can; it's not as strong as some others on the album, but it's still interesting enough.

After the two uncommon lovers of "For You," the cast of misfits in "Spirit in the Night" are refreshing and wholesome. Mostly refreshing; Crazy Janey and her mission man, Wild Billy with his friend G-man, and Hazy Davy and Killer Joe sound like critters worth hanging out with. In fact, this is the most straightforward, essentially innocent song on side two. It's just a hedonistic Saturday night up at Greasy Lake, "about a mile down on the dark side of route 48."

Nothing much to fret about; Clarence keeps things cool and loose with his sax—this is really his finest moment on *Greetings*. Of course, "Hazy Davy got really hurt, he ran into the lake in just his socks and his shirt," but everyone else is doin' swell, especially Bruce and Crazy Janey, makin' love in the dirt." Nothing tough or cryptic or difficult to swallow about the jazzy "Spirit in the Night"; it's light and airy and just fine.

"It's Hard to Be a Saint in the City" is the song Bruce first played on that fateful day in John Hammond's office, and it's easy to understand why he got the job. Of the many tales of New Jersey-New York street life Springsteen spins on *Greetings* this is the most enticing and appealing.

It's Bruce just the way his fans would picture him. Dave Sancious' piano intro is appro-

> Greetings was a shot in the arm jaded rock fans needed so desperately in 1973.

priately slithery for a singer who tells us "I had skin like leather and the diamond-hard look of a cobra . . . I could walk like Brando right into the sun, Then dance just like a Casanova." Here's a guy who can strut down the street and hear its heart beat.

This guy's brimming over with confidence, positively oozing street smarts. He knows this turf and he's in command; he knows all its secular temptations and he isn't particularly upset that "It's Hard to be a Saint in the City."

Bruce closes out *Greetings from Asbury Park, N.J.* in strong fashion with this tune, which captures the essence of much of what has gone before it. It is proud, youthful, urban, and urbane, and it is what the 1972-73 Bruce is all about.

Greetings from Asbury Park N.J. is a stunner, but not without its limitations. There are occasions when you wish Bruce was a little disciplined in his verbiage, but at the time you'd be wary of putting any restraints on a man who can conjure up so many vivid pictures. And the music is just fine, if a bit sparse; David Sancious is particularly out-

CHUCK PULIN

BOBBY BANK

> *The "new Dylan" tag on Springsteen began early; indeed it was so prevalent that Dylan was at times referred to as "the old Springsteen."*

standing on this disc. Still, it's a lot thinner than Bruce wanted, and it might not be an accurate reflection of where he was at musically at the time.

The most important matter remains, however, that *Greetings* was a shot in the arm jaded rock fans needed so desperately in 1973 Springsteen set his sights high and didn't get the whole enchilada but he got plenty. In the process, he re-established lofty standards for composition and vocal interpretation. In a period when sloth was the predominant art form, this is anything but a lazy album.

Of the music on *Greetings*, *Crawdaddy* editor Peter Knobler said, "I hadn't felt this kind of hard edge intelligent lunatic intensity since *Blonde on Blonde*."

"There hasn't been an album like this in ages," wrote Knobler. "There are individual lines worth entire records. There is the combined sensibility of the chaser and the chaste, the street punk and the book worm. The record rocks, then glides, then rocks again."

Just after the release of *Greetings* and the early cult and critical reception, Bruce would tell Knobler, "I'm at a place now where I'm flattered. I'm flattered and I'm happy that people would take an interest, you know? You have to watch out, though. You don't want to get too self-centered. It's easy to do, you know, because people are always shovin' you in your face."

Respected rock critic Langdon Winner was later to call *Greetings* "an elaborate mess —sprawling, incoherent, lacking any real center of gravity. The thing that stuck in my mind was the verbiage that poured from each song. It was as if my *American Heritage Dictionary* had sprung a leak, flooding the living room with nouns and adjectives."

With the debut album out, Springsteen, as many new acts do, performed at the annual Columbia Records con-

vention in the summer of '73. The appearance was said to be less than auspicious. "It was during a period when he physically looked like Dylan," John Hammond observed afterward. "He came on with a chip on his shoulder and played too long. People came up to me and said, 'He really can't be that bad, can he, John?' "

The "new Dylan" tag on Springsteen began early; indeed, it was so prevalent that Dylan, before his resurgence with *Blood On The Tracks* in 1974, was at times referred to as "the old Springsteen."

The recording industry has been looking for another Dylan for several years, almost as feverishly as they seek "the new Beatles." In fact, another in a line of "new Dylans," Mississippi singer-songwriter Steve Forbert, is being promoted by Columbia Records at this very moment.

Columbia signed Bruce as an acoustic folk act; *Greetings from Asbury Park, N.J.* was originally pegged as a non-electric album. In their enthusiasm about Bruce's songwriting ability, Columbia officials had neglected a few facts about his performing career.

It was true that he was a solo acoustic act at the time he was brought to John Hammond, but that situation had only existed for a short spell because Bruce could not financially support a backup band.

"I told them I'd been playing in bands for eight years and by myself for two-three months," Springsteen explained in his first *Crawdaddy* interview in March, 1973.

"They forgot about the eight years and went with the two months." He told one reporter "I had to fight to get what band was on there."

Springsteen addressed the matter head on at the very beginning. For Dylan he had only praise. "It's *the* greatest music ever written, to me. The man says it all, exactly the right way. Incredibly powerful. You don't get no more intense. Such a great instrumental sound. And he was . . . he was Bob Dylan, you know?

"But it's like a map," Springsteen observed. "You gotta read a map. You just can't go off in the middle of the woods and go off in the right direction. You don't so you've gotta look. You've gotta say, I dig the way the cat's doing it; I want to do it like that, but . . . like this."

He added, "I go onstage and feel myself. And I'm not worrying about 'oh man that note sounds like this dude. Hey man, I heard that word off of *Subterranean Homesick Blues'!* At one time it worried me but it doesn't anymore, because when I get onstage finally I feel myself. That's who I am."

"I like the cat," Springsteen said of Dylan on another occasion. "But we come from two totally different scenes, you gotta remember that." He told *Rolling Stone* reporter Pat Knight in Texas; "I've been influence by a lot of people. Elvis was one of the first. Otis Redding, Sam Cooke, Wilson Pickett, the Beatles, Fats [Domino], Benny Goodman, a lot of jazz guys. You can hear them all in there if you want.

Bruce, who believes Chuck Berry was one of the great rock lyricists, told one reporter that his attraction to Dylan was not primarily lyrical. "I would say that it was originally Dylan—'Like a Rolling Stone.' I heard that on the radio. At first, I didn't hear the lyrics at all. I just heard the chorus, 'Like a rollin' stone . . .' That was the important part."

Imitating the song's opening drum and organ parts with his hands and voice,

> "I go onstage and feel myself. And I'm not worrying about 'oh man that note sounds like this dude. At one time it worried me but it doesn't anymore, because when I get onstage finally I feel myself. That's who I am.'"

Bruce went on, "and, the band would roll in. It was great. And, that was the first thing I knew about Dylan." It causes one to wonder how much of a difference Mike Bloomfield and Al Kooper would have made on *Greetings from Asbury Park, N.J.*

It's also interesting to note that Bob Johnston, who produced *Highway 61 Revisted, John Wesley Harding,* and *Blonde on Blonde,* three of Dylan's finest achievements, indicated early in Bruce's career that he would like to produce for him. Johnston said he'd just let Bruce play, watch the tapes roll, and catch what went down.

Even with *Greetings* out, E Street living did not become easy street. On the first trip to play in Boston, Bruce and the boys stayed in a friend's attic. There were only four mattresses, "so every night after the gig we had to try to figure out whose turn it was to sleep on the floor."

Bruce, however, does not look on those as bad times. "It was never a down," he explained in *Creem*. "Me and Steve would always sit back and say, 'As bad as this is right now, it will never be as bad as it was before we made an album or got a break.' Who are we to complain. This is easy street. I'm lucky number one." He observed, "it's a lot of work, but you're doing something you like. We always considered ourselves to be way in front with the whole ball game."

The second album was not long in the waiting. *The Wild, the Innocent, and the E Street Shuffle* appeared in November. Playing live to promote the first album, Bruce had begun to reassemble a band, some from the old days and a newcomer or two, but all New Jersey boys.

Columbia had finally realized Bruce was not a solo acoustic act; *The E Street Shuffle* was his second record but it was really the first vinyl representation of anything resembling the E Street Band as we now know it. Bruce finally got the full instrumentation he wanted for this one.

As a result, *The E Street Shuffle* puts more emphasis on musicianship and ensemble playing. It is not nearly as lyrically frenetic as *Greetings*, and, perhaps because he felt folks were paying too much attention to his words, this is the only Springsteen album without printed lyrics provided for the purchaser.

The first cut is enough of an introduction to the Springsteen mythology for anyone who may be joining him for the first time. In a way, Bruce is like the stage manager in the play *Our Town*, as he guides his audience past a panorama of his town's most notable citizens.

The difference is that this ain't quaint little Grovers Corners, N.H.; it's hot and sticky Asbury Park, N.J., where there are no quilting bees; stage manager Springsteen lets us know that the natives have pulled "all stops out on a Friday night."

The cut, "E Street Shuffle," begins with Bruce's hastily assembled "oompah" band, Vini Lopez on cornet and Garry Tellent on tuba (is he this band's John Entwistle?), with enough missed notes and musical flatulence to suit a beer drinking Friday on the boardwalk.

"Sparks fly on E Street," the Boss begins as he brings the oompahs to a close with his guitar, and they certainly do. This is one of those sound of the city tunes with plenty of bedlam in the background, voices blabbering behind Bruce's narration. It's a good bet he's talking about himself when he sings "the boy prophet's walking handsome and hot" as he observes nightly goings on in a boardwalk world where just about everybody's full-time job seems to be staying one step in front of the law. And a woman's major preoccupation seems to be keeping "those crazy boys out of trouble." With keyboard player Dave Sancious adding soprano sax to Clarence's tenor and Lopez and Tallent, this is one of Bruce's most raucous tunes; it's probably the most brass he's ever had on one song, especially with the guest appearance of Albany "Al" Tellone from Newark on baritone sax.

This is a loud night on the boardwalk he's talking about, so not everything is clear and simple, least of all the music. The band is muddled and garbled, but here, at least, it's intentional. It's quite a din Bruce sings above here; welcome to E Street, and hang on to your hat.

"The E Street Shuffle" makes for a fine rock overture, a perfect thematic summation of what we are about to hear. The elements of Bruce's Asbury Park are all there in a jumble on the opening track; they will be sorted out on the subsequent songs.

The next of these is "4th of July, Asbury Park (Sandy)," usually referred to as "Sandy." It's a romantic evening on the boardwalk; if we didn't already know it Bruce's sweetly arranged guitar and mandolin opening would tell us as much.

"Sandy" shows Bruce in a reflective mood. "The fireworks are hailing over little Eden" and everyone should be snuggling with their sweetie, but hardly anyone is. The fireworks force a light "into all those stony faces left stranded on this warm July." Greasers sleep on beaches; anxious studs open their shirts to display their chests and busy themselves "chasing all them silly New York virgins by the score."

Bruce himself has problems, too; a waitress has lost her desire for him and "chasing the factory girls underneath the boardwalk where they promise to unsnap their jeans" apparently doesn't pay off.

Futile, fruitless, and unful- filling, it would seem, and on this night the boy prophet wants to change it all. He's tired of dusty arcades and "banging them pleasure ma-

chines." These woes are confessed to Sandy, who happens to be with him this particular night and whom he wants to "love me tonight for I may never see you again."

Boy prophet views more of the sorry evening and swears "for me this boardwalk life's through, babe; you oughtta quit this scene, too." And now he's got a better reason for her; "love me tonight and I promise I'll love you forever." But forever comes out

DAVID GAHR

of his mouth like a question; like Meat Loaf in "Paradise by Dashboard Light" he's put himself in this spot, but he doesn't back off; "Yeah, I mean it Sandy Girl," he swears.

"Sandy" is a haunting, totally effective song, another side of Bruce; this is the dark side of the exhuberance of "The E Street Shuffle." His existence suddenly strikes him as empty, and he reaches out to the person closest at hand. He's willing to promise anything.

There's a melancholy beauty to it all; Bruce's guitar underpins his singing, and this is some of the first evidence that Bruce was truly developing as a vocalist. His voice sings poetry but betrays pain; he implores; he whispers when he is too overwhelmed to speak. This is a soft, somber tune, and Bruce's voice conveys all the feelings this

brilliant composition requires.

The quiet beauty of "Sandy" is a necessary respite between "E Street Shuffle" and the high voltage of "Kitty's Back," a longtime concert showstopper. This is perhaps the most street-smart, fingersnapping hip song on the album; and the music that carries that smartness is a hybrid of Eddie Cochran and Sam and Dave, if one can imagine such a thing. The folks who stood up and took notice of Bruce did so because of songs like this one. It cooks, to use a word one has little reason to use in writing about music anymore. The guys in "Kitty's Back" will tell you their problems but they really haven't got anything that *they* would call problems. They exist for the sheer joy of being alive; and the music on "Kitty's Back" was made for the sheer joy of making it. It 1973, who else

was doing that?

There's a long drawling guitar intro by Bruce to show that he can do that, and then begins the tale of Kitty, obviously the hippest chick in town: "she'll have to marry some top cat, ain't it the cool truth."

The only problem is that she's not *in* town, but word has it that she's coming back, and that's reason enough to play with delightful but reckless abandon.

In their biggest instrumental workout on record to date, Bruce's mates achieved mixed success. This is brisk, exuberant stuff that makes guys who haven't gotten out of their seats since Altamont get out of their seats even if they're sitting at home.

Of course, if you listen a few times, you'll notice the missed notes, the sudden tempo changes in appropriate places, and the thudding foot

pedal of Vini Lopez. But you can also notice how these guys work to such a furious state that they have to come tumbling down, in a kind of musical whirlpool out of which comes a real tasty organ solo by Sancious, who at this point rivaled Clarence as the band's top player.

You begin to realize how, in his early material, you really depend on a lyric sheet from Bruce. In this maelstrom, you can only pick out a few lines, some just 'cause they sound great. "There hasn't been a tally since Sally left the alley" is cause for consternation even if we don't know what hasn't been tallied or who Sally is or where the alley is located. And "you better let them move fast when they're young" is pretty much the story of Springsteen's adolescence, and just about everybody's.

Prodigal daughter Kitty does come back, by the way, and the heralds announcing her arrival are Bruce and his band. "God knows this Kitty's been untrue, like she left for a city dude," but Springsteen knows that with some women a lot can be forgiven. "She's so soft, she's so blue, when he looks into her eyes [he] just sits back and sighs 'ooh ooh, what can I do?' " What indeed? Give Clarence a solo. He takes it, and "Kitty's Back" on the wings of his sax.

There was once an album called *Have a Rave Up* with the Yardbirds; we have just had a rave up with Bruce and the lads and for ears turning to mellow marshmallows it was long overdue. Thanks, Bruce.

In jazz, there is always talk of the "cool" and "hot" schools of music; on *The Wild, the Innocent, and the E Street Shuffle*, Bruce gives us hot and cool in a masterful bal-ance. After the fiery "Kitty's Back" comes the sedate and somber "Wild Billy's Circus Story."

This is not one of Bruce's most frequently heard songs, but it does show another interesting side of him (is he hexagonal? octagonal?). With an accordion and tuba intro, the song sounds physically heavy, as if the narrator (Bruce) is either trying to follow the proceedings with weights strapped to his legs or from the midst of a dense mental fog.

The circus unfolds like one of Bruce's Breughelian landscapes; it's a colorful scene but a hard life. "The fire-eater's lyin' in a pool of sweat, victim of the heat wave," and "fat lady, big mama, Mrs. Bimbo sits in her chair and yawns." Bruce counts off the acrobatic Margarita's neck twists on the high wire, and "the elephants dance real funky" to the accompaniment of Garry Tallent's tuba.

But the circus life isn't for everyone. One fellow can't take the loneliness; he departs in the middle of the night as the carnival sounds haunt him on the highway. Bruce implores the Lord, "send some good women to save all your clowns."

"Circus Story" is a richly textured track, a remarkably hearty sound considering it's mostly just the voice and the acoustic guitar of Bruce. His visual imagery gives us plenty to latch on to, and he extracts enough color and flourish from his guitar that we almost don't notice that the band has disappeared. We may have strayed a ways from E Street with this song, but it's still a fine epilogue to side one or, if you prefer, an intermission before side two.

Two years later, when *Born to Run* would be released, one critic would note that some of Bruce's songs were so dazzling, so moving, so involving that it was almost impossible to listen to them without weeping.

He could have made that comment two years earlier in talking about "Incident on 57th Street," easily the best song on *The Wild, the Innocent, and the E Street Shuffle*, a real stunner of the kind of pretty-ugly beauty Bruce is so capable of conveying. I almost hesitate to describe his earlier songs as poetry, because what does that leave for this masterpiece? As inflated as Appel's comparisons of Springsteen to Keats, Springsteen to Byron might sound, I'd dare anyone to match the pathos of "Incident on 57th Street."

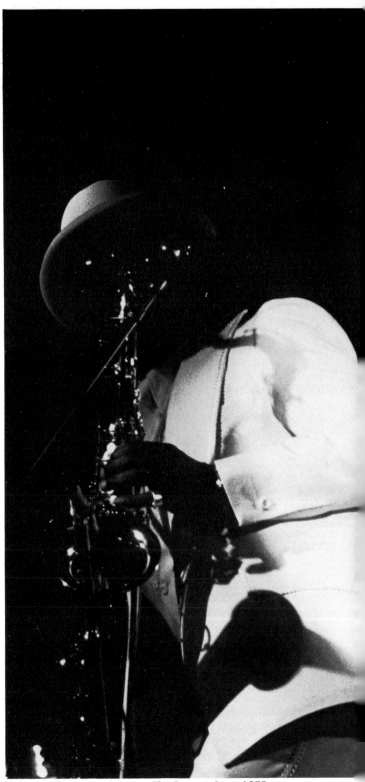

Clarence Clemons and Bruce, The Bottom Line, 1975

38

CHUCK PULIN

Pianist Sancious is a hero here; he plays piano behind Bruce like a lutenist would accompany Shakespeare. The saga begins when "Spanish Johnny drove in from the underworld last night/with bruised arms and broken rhythm and a beat up old Buick but just dressed like dynamite."

He's in town "to try and sell his heart" but the whores tell him "Johnny, it falls apart so easily and you know these days hearts are so cheap." All is lost until Puerto Rican Jane emerges from the shadows and consoles him, "Johnny, don't cry."

Johnny ("like a cool Romeo he'd made his moves") wants to drive her to the other side of town "where paradise ain't so crowded." He's full of big notions, this Johnny.

Yet, as in "Sandy," the character seems to realize that this is an environment that's seen better days. The next verse is one of Bruce's finest:

Johnny was sitting on the fire escape watching the kids play down the street;

He called down 'hey little hero, summer's long but I guess it ain't very sweet a-round here anymore';

Jane sleeps in sheets damp with sweat, Johnny sits up alone and watches her dream on, dream on;

And his sister prays for lost souls, then breaks down in the chapel after everyone's gone;

Jane moves over to share her pillow but opens her eyes to see Johnny up and putting his clothes on.

For the moment she's lost him to the "romantic young boys" who call from outside "hey Spanish Johnny, wanna make some easy money?" In hushed tones Johnny swears "Goodnight, it's alright Jane/ I'll meet you tomorrow night on Lover's Lane." He promises "we may walk until daylight maybe;" from the mouth of Springsteen it is a cry for freedom, and maybe they'll do that, and maybe that'll solve everthing.

"Incident" is also a great vocal display for the Boss. As the omniscient observer he is wise, almost whiskey-voiced even if he doesn't drink. As Jane of course he's sweet and soft, and as Johnny he sends chills up your spine; Johnny alternates between dire reve-

be young and rootless and electric."

"Rosalita" also finds Bruce in his least ambivalent mood on the entire album. There are no doubts; Rosie's the one, "the only lover I'm ever gonna need," and he boasts "I ain't here on business baby, I'm only here for fun." Somewhat cryptically, he assures her "you don't have to call me lieutenant."

As the Latin riffs of the Big Man's saxophone serenade Rosie, Bruce acknowledges that this relationship has problems; her mama don't like him "cause I play in a rock 'n' roll band" and her dad don't dig him cause "he never did understand." He also is under the impression that the man who would dare steal his

named Jack the Rabbit, Weak-Kneed Willy, Sloppy Sue, and Big Balls Billy, and a car headed to a small cafe in California. And he's got the Big Man wailing on the saxophone!

This is Clarence's showcase on the second album, and in seven minutes there's plenty of time to blow off steam. Bruce has shown us a good deal of the dark edge, and the gray fringes, of his existence on this record; now he gives us 100 percent pure "it's good to be alive and me" music. Small wonder that this has been a long time concert favorite of the band and its audience.

Everybody needs a rest after that one, so the album's closer, "New York Serenade," is a lullaby by comparison.

> "I ain't here on business baby, I'm only here for fun."

lation, impassioned assurances, and desperate pleas, and Bruce truly brings this boy to life. "Incident on 57th Street" is worth the price of admission; it may leave you trembling in a cold sweat.

Relief is up next in the tumultuous form of "Rosalita," which could easily be called "The Wild and the Reckless" by the way Bruce, Clarence and the rest deliver seven hot and sweaty minutes of all get out. The very nature of the music says "ain't it great to

daughter is seriously lacking in cash.

None of this bothers the man with a mission. If success is sweet revenge, then Bruce is all set. "Tell him this is his last chance to get his daughter in a fine romance," he sings jubilantly, "because the record company, Rosie, just gave me a big advance."

"Rosalita" is pure frenzied joy. The Bruce who sings this song has everything he wants: a dreamy chiquita, a record contract, a bunch of buddies

The openings belong to Sancious, in a solo that combines classical passages with jazz phrasings in a sort of wedding of Rachmaninoff and Ellington. Bruce even picks a little mandolin on this one about an evening excursion to the other side of the Hudson River. "It's midnight in Manhattan, this is no time to get cute; it's a mad dog's promenade." Maybe, but there are too many elements at work here to get a grip on. There are lush strings, ar-

40

ranged by Sancious; besides "Jungleland," this is the only presence of violins yet on a Springsteen cut. The story here does not move us nor is it on the move; there's a lot the scope of his performing talent. On the basis of this second effort, folks could get a pretty good idea of what to expect from a Bruce Springsteen concert. *Greetings* gave enjoy nor understand its sprawling range and seemingly endless variety, so the whole thing just made me nervous: too many changes, no sustained melodies, no con-

> ## "Ain't it great to be young and rootless and electric."

about "New York Serenade" that says "this is the coda, after which we're through," but in more than nine minutes of vinyl little is resolved lyrically or musically. This serenade is an anticlimax.

The Wild, the Innocent, and the E Street Shuffle is far from perfect. The production hardly befits the creative input; the performing talents could certainly be sorted out better. Some tracks go on for too long, others stray a bit in the middle.

Yet there is enough with which to evaluate Bruce Springsteen and welcome him as something close to a messiah in the rock world. There's vibrant, energetic ensemble playing here, which is what rock and roll was supposed to be about all along. And the lyrical strength displayed on "Sandy" and "Incident on 57th Street" shoots Bruce right into the front ranks of rhyme makers.

E Street Shuffle is also an important step for Springsteen because it is really the first record to truly indicate

them no such indication.

Bruce called his second release "a lazy hanging-out summer album." And what was this wild and innocent place called E Street anyway? E Street in Asbury Park was in fact the home address of keyboard player Dave Sancious, but whether the song "The E Street Shuffle" or the name E Street Band came first is a matter of confusion even to Springsteen.

The album came out of "the summer the band consciousness started to develop," Bruce remembers. "We were just sitting there, flashing on everything that was happening. I was exactly where I wanted to be. I had a band. I knew who I was. We were getting work. The album reflects that."

The public reaction to *The Wild, the Innocent, and the E Street Shuffle* was similar to that of *New Times* writer Janet Maslin, who later observed, "I knew *E Street Shuffle* was good from the first, and I certainly knew it was different. But I could neither

ventional structure, no explanation of why everybody's so glad that Kitty's back. (Rosalita, with its sly humor and a horn line so torrid it could move even a mathematician to mambo, was an immediately accessible exception.)

Maslin noted, "If *E Street Shuffle* is wildly exciting, it's also a little wild; the arrangements hinge on constant surprises, the lyrics are full of evocative but disjointed imagery, the mood is often indistinct yet always shifting."

Rock writer Stan Mieses saw Bruce's second effort as a considerable step forward from the first. *Greetings,* he felt, "in many ways only told you as much about the place and the person as a glossy snapshot might. The follow-up, he said, was "like watching a still picture suddenly become a movie."

"It should be dance music," Bruce told Mieses. "It's a very alive feeling I try to get into the songs—no matter what the situation. The people in the songs are alive."

41

And they're still New Jersey seaside characters; "I'm still drawing from the place," he said of his boardwalk haunts. "It's got everything for me."

Although it actually came out at the end of '73, *The Wild, the Innocent and the E Street Shuffle* was named by *Rolling Stone* as one of the seven best albums of 1974. In *Melody Maker*, Michael Watts effused in 1974 "I listen to Springsteen like I used to listen to Dylan, John Lennon, and Chuck Berry—as though a life depended on it."

Even with two albums behind him, Springsteen had done very little touring outside the East; this may have had more to do with his slow climb to success than is generally noted.

Bruce had made two stipulations that limited touring possibilities. First, he didn't want to go near huge arenas with the fifteen- to twenty-thousand seat capacities. And secondly, he didn't want to open for anyone; he wanted to be the headliner.

He was touring more by 1974, however. In the fall, Bruce set out to expand his turf with a southern spin (the boys traveled by Amtrak) that included Washington, D.C., Houston, and Austin, Texas.

The results were as shattering as they so often were back home. Folks who didn't know this New Jersey boy from Adam were giving him one standing ovation after another, just begging him to stay for just one more song.

After one Texas triumph, organist Danny Federici explained "we've done gigs around the Southeast and New England. Went to Chicago once. Single gigs to see what a tour might look like."

According to Federici, having Bruce as the headliner was not just the Boss' idea. "We talked to some big names about opening tour shows for them, but, uh, some people won't play after us. They must think we're too strong to follow."

There was one early tour with Chicago which Bruce remembers as a horrendous enterprise. "We had the problem of any opening act playing in twenty thousand-seat halls. They just won't listen to you. They can't hear, for one thing. They don't know how to listen, for another. Some groups just go out and plow through it. But I can't do it that way. And it showed—we played thirteen or fourteen gigs in them big halls and we sold no records. We didn't start sellin' records until we started playin' smaller places. It's a slow process. But I was *always* certain. I was just sure about what I was doin'."

The month *Greetings* was released, Bruce had opened for David Bromberg at Pall's Mall in Boston; all concerned admitted it was a horror show. Later in the year he played a Central Park concert billed between Anne Murray and Brewer and Shipley. It is unlikely that their fans could appreciate what Bruce was doing up there.

For awhile at the end of '74, the regular E Street lineup was complemented by the presence of a softening influence. She was Suki Lahav, quite blonde and very ethereal, and she played lilting and langorous violin. Sort of like Scarlet Rivera to Bruce's

Bob Dylan. Lahav's stay was all too brief: she had to return to Israel.

WMMR in Philadelphia had been one of the first stations to play *Greetings* and gave *The Wild, the Innocent and the E Street Shuffle* decent airplay when it came out in November of the same year. But the City of Brotherly Love embraced its neighbor from the north like a long lost son; by 1974 *Wild and Innocent* was the most played album in WMMR's history.

The station's Ed Sciaky, who is also a print journalist, has seen Springsteen in concert at least 100 times from coast to coast. He has been known to ask "are you ready to accept Bruce Springsteen as your personal savior?"

Ed recalled as he drove to a Baltimore show with *Happytimes* reporter Cinnie Morgan in 1976 "I saw Bruce in April of '73 at the Main Point. I may have seen him once before that. I saw him at the Spectrum when he opened for Chicago in June of '73, but he was terrible. In terms of everything else that was happening at the time, it was good but it wasn't like he was God yet."

In reviewing a Springsteen show at The Main Point in Bryn Mawr early in 1975, Sciaky called Sprintsteen "*the* most exciting thing to happen to rock and roll *ever*," and denied that he was falling victim to hyperbole or hype. "People get so overwhelmed by his performances that they become raving maniacs," Sciaky explained.

To Ed, Springsteen "is the single most magnetic, most believable actor-singer-musician you'll ever see. I mean, he makes you laugh and cry and scream your head off as he makes his songs' characters and situations come to life in front of you."

The Main Point, one of the most prestigious of the smaller folk-rock clubs in this country, was an important edifice in Springsteen's career. It was one of the first venues outside New Jersey that he ever played; very close to the day *Greetings from Asbury Park, N.J.* was released, Bruce was at The Main Point on the bottom of a bill behind a Boston comedy act, Travis Shook and the Club Wow.

Very little has been written about it, but those who marvel at Springsteen's rich and visual imagery and his brilliantly drawn characters are always wondering what this man's literary influences were. They might be disappointed; a couple of years ago he told a writer that the last two books he'd read were *The Exorcist* and *The Godfather.*

In *Hit Parader,* Joseph Rose quoted Springsteen as saying "I don't have time to read books. You know what it's like. I don't have patience either. That's my problem. If I get into reading them, I like to read them. But I can't sit there and take all them hours reading a book."

Bruce reflected, "That was my problem in school. I couldn't stand reading them books. Not that I didn't like them. I just didn't have the patience to do it. Because, like, if something's going to happen, I like to make it happen. Like if I want to do a song, I want to do it right now."

On another occasion he explained, "I wasn't brought up in a house where there was a lot of reading and stuff. I was brought up on TV. Who was William Burroughs? They never brought him up in high school in the '60s. Unless you hung around with that kind of crowd—and I didn't hang around with no crowd that was talking about William Burroughs."

As articulate in a streetwise way as he may be, Bruce is hardly a man for sedentary

CHARLYN ZLOTNIK

MICHAEL PUTLAND / RETNA

pursuits. He is the quintessential man of action. His literature is the environment he chooses; his influences are whatever his eyes and ears pick up.

And to listen to him tell it, it doesn't much matter where he catches those glimpses; he's not wedded to one place. "I don't know how important the settings are in the first place," Bruce told John Rockwell in a *Rolling Stone* piece. "It could be New Jersey, it could be California, it could be Alaska. The images are like the coloring, not necessarily the picture. I can float anywhere—uptown, downtown, anywhere. I want to do everything. I want to see everything, I want to go everywhere."

It is almost impossible to believe that a man who has come to epitomize joyous exuberance and swift, spontaneous, off-the-wall action neither drinks, uses drugs, nor cusses in front of ladies.

Apparently it was always that way. Responding to a question from *Good Times* reporter Susan Ahrens, Bruce once explained, "Was I straight? That's all there was at the time. There were groups like the rahrahs and the greasers, and I bounced back and forth, trying to figure out where I fit in, 'til I found out I *didn't* fit in. I didn't dig the scene that either had happening. So consequently I didn't do anything; I just kinda was."

One thing he definitely *never* was is a gastronome. One of the areas in which Bruce has remained quite faithful to his humble, scuffling roots is his diet. It's unlikely you will ever see The Boss nibbling on

CHUCK PULIN

pate de foie gras or ordering from a wine list with any degree of expertise.

The man apparently lives on burgers—three meals a day of them, by some accounts. He knows how crazy that is; he even makes fun of it.

In a 1974 concert in Austin, Texas, (one of the first areas outside of the East Coast where Bruce became popular), he concluded a sparkling set with "Twist and Shout," fi-

highest annual consumption, right behind *Playboy* publisher Hugh Hefner. In the days when they were still less than household words, Bruce and his E Street pals used to play long games of Monopoly, which is based on life in another boardwalk town up the road apiece, Atlantic City. Dylan, "America has never produced another performer who uses the rock beat, uses words intelligently, observes

which showed early good taste by treating him like a major star before any other

Bruce would show up for games loaded down with enough Pepsi and Drake's cakes to nourish the whole band. But he had come to conquer the Monopoly board and wasn't giving anything away. If you wanted a Pepsi, he'd give you one in exchange for a hotel.

By the beginning of '75,

> *The man apparently lives on burgers— three meals a day of them, by some accounts. He knows how crazy that is; he even makes fun of it.*

nally falling to the floor in mock collapse.

Clutching his chest, the singer told the Texans "my doctor told me not to play 'Twist and Shout' tonight. See, I eat a lot of cheeseburgers, got a lot of cholesterol around my heart. I don't think I can do it one more time." But he did, of course, in bravura fashion.

Pepsis are apparently another Springsteen passion. Among the famous, he probably manages the second

his entire environment, and cares enough about the environment to mold these observations into music. Not one. Except Bruce Springsteen.

"He confronts this ugliness and celebrates it," the review noted. "He does not ask how one can change this environment, but rather how one can cope with it . . . Like J.D. Salinger's characters, Springsteen's are eternal adolescents."

And they loved him more than ever in Philadelphia,

Bruce was an important enough rock figure and a strong enough critical favorite for plenty of people to agree with *The Insider,* which observed that with the exception of city did. In 1975 he was back at the Main Point to pay his respects with a single benefit show for the club. WMMR was to tape and later broadcast the performance.

That was Springsteen's seventh appearance at the Main Point since the Travis Shook date. His eighth was a

few months later, when he
guested on stage with Jackson
Browne, who had first played
at the 270-seat club in 1971.
Browne invited Bruce up to
join David Lindley and him
for acoustic versions of
"Thunder Road" and "Born
To Run."

Bruce's following may have
been rabid but it was not
large enough to suit some fac-
tions at Columbia Records.
1974 and the first few months
of 1975 came and went without a third album from Springsteen. Clive Davis was no
longer at the company, and in
some circles Bruce had been
considered Davis' boy. Not
everyone at Columbia was as
enchanted with Springsteen,
nor were they as patient as
Davis. They wanted a new album, and they wanted a single to help sell the album.

In Cleveland for a concert
at John Carroll University in
March, Bruce was asked by a
writer for *Exit* about the long
stretch between albums.

"I just like . . . I don't run
what I do on a deadline. I
mean, I just don't do that,
you know."

He had heard hundreds of
times that a third album was
needed to keep his slowly es-
calating popularity from
petering out, but Bruce was
still doing concerts, convert-
ing a few hundred or thousand
listeners along the way, and
didn't seem panicked.

"It is coming around. It's
coming around as slow as the
hills, but that's OK, 'cause
I'm not in any big rush or
nothin'. I'd rather sort of be
this way, maybe. I never say,
'Gee whiz, why didn't they
buy that album?' Like, we
sold 100,000 records or something. That's a lot to me, you

Clarence and Bruce,
Paramount Theatre, Oakland, 1975

ALLEN TANNENBAUM

know. Even though it may not be a lot to other people."

Bruce knew what people were saying and thinking. "People run out and say, 'I gotta make a record.' You don't. You make a record when you want to make a record, and when you're ready to make a record. It's been over a year, so what? We just don't run in the studio and waste our time. There's too much junk out already. There's no point in throwin' out more junk, you know?"

In a 1974 interview with *Sounds,* Bruce had revealed that the third record would be "not actually a concept type thing, but it's like you get a jigsaw puzzle and you put it down on the floor and it slowly comes together." It would feature "songs around a feeling, a mood. It's going to need more instruments than the other albums to get that feel, but it can be done."

Bruce was more than a little perturbed at the pressure to produce a hit single. "I'm not going to quit on them," he said of his record company. I'm going to be making music for the rest of my life! There's nothing else I want to do. There's nothing else I can do.

"And now they want a single instead of my album," he exclaimed. "Did they ask Michelangelo to paint them a picture of his parents before he could do the Sistine Chapel?"

"I can't be pressured," Bruce told another reporter. "When it's ready, it'll be there. I decided a long time ago that I know who I am and where I came from. And I know what it is to get caught up in that pressure—you start thinking that you're something else,

49

you become a product of the entertainment business. I try to keep my perspective on the thing. It's even for the good of the record company that I do that, because I'll give them my best, and it'll work out for the best in the end."

At this crucial point in Springsteen's career, Jon Landau sprang up and helped save the day and get the third album, *Born to Run*, off and running.

Landau's assistance was only fitting. In many ways, he had put the pressure on Bruce to fully realize his "rock star" potential.

Landau had been the most important voice to warn listeners of the coming of Bruce. A longtime *Rolling Stone* editor, he was perhaps the most articulate, perceptive, and trusted rock critic in the land.

Landau caught a Springsteen show in Cambridge; it was one of those fateful moments. Not one to go out on a limb, Landau nevertheless coined the phrase that was to be a boon and a curse alike to Bruce, the words that rally Bruce's fans and enrage his detractors. In Boston's *Real Paper*, Landau acknowledged "I have seen the future of rock and roll and it's name is Bruce Springsteen."

The *Real Paper* review continued "on a night when I needed to feel young, he made me feel like I was hearing music for the very first time. When his two-hour set ended I could only think, can anyone be this good, can anyone say this much to me, can rock 'n' roll still speak with this kind of glory?"

He added "tonight there is someone I can write of the way I used to write, without reservations of any kind. Last Thursday . . . I saw my rock 'n' roll past flash before my eyes . . . Last Thursday I remembered that the magic still exists."

In the beginning, the 'future of rock and roll" didn't mind the epithet at all. "Landau's quote helped reaffirm a belief in myself," Bruce has since said. "The band and I were making fifty dollars a week. It helped me go on. I realized I was gettin' through to somebody."

Later, when Bruce was reading another Landau review in the window of a Cambridge club, he was approached by none other than the reviewer himself. "I wrote that review," Landau modestly stated. He and Bruce got to talking and became fast friends. Meanwhile, Columbia fashioned an entire advertising campaign around Landau's quote.

Landau was the cavalry that was to be called in when the sessions for Springsteen's third album stopped making progress altogether. At tiny 914 Studios in Blauvelt, N.Y., where the first two albums had been recorded, Bruce had completed just one track, "Born to Run" itself. Tapes of the track were circulated to New York, Boston, Philadelphia, and Cleveland stations. Response was positive; interest in Springsteen was mushrooming. But to make it really happen, to break out beyond cult status, Bruce and The E Streeters needed a third album.

At 914 one night, the band went through the lengthy and complex "Jungleland" fourteen consecutive times without a take deemed usable by the Boss.

"I've always had songs going into the studio," Bruce told *Crawdaddy,* and once I've gotten in there something always started going in me and I'd write some more." It was essentially a holding pattern at 914 Studios while Bruce struggled to come to grips with his material.

Help was needed and it came in the form of Landau. With Bruce and Appel, Landau signed on as a co-producer. His previous production credits, albums for Detroit's MC5 and for Livingston Taylor, were duds. Production wasn't really what he was there for—Bruce could handle that. What these guys needed was motivation from the outside, from someone who hadn't been bogged down with the rest of them. One of Landau's first suggestions, one that was heeded, was that the entire operation be moved to the more expensive, but more sophisticated and perhaps more inspiring Record Plant in New York City.

"The biggest thing Landau did was to make me see that I was screwing up," Springsteen later explained to Peter Knobler. Once he began to work in earnest, Springsteen finished writing most of the *Born to Run* material in about three weeks. The breakthrough came when he drastically altered his approach to song writing.

"My mistake was in attempting to write in a particular way I had written *before,* you know, instead of looking to go a slightly different way," he explained. "I know in the end I took a different approach toward some of the lyrics in the songs. If you read them on paper some-

times they don't look that good, but when you hear them they've got the right *feel.*"

The single track "Born to Run" had taken him six months to write. To hear him tell it, song writing is tantamount to torture. "I was fighting myself all the time, you know. Always do that. Everybody's hard on themselves; well I take it to an extreme sometimes, where it starts like being self-defeating. In a way it's good, because I think in the end you do pull out the best stuff, but it's really a mind-breaking project. It'll freak you out. You get frustrated and you go nuts."

By the time operations were moved to the Record Plant, the E Street Band lineup had become essentially what it is today. Drummer Vini Lopez had departed some time ago. Ernest "Boom" Carter had sat in on drums for the 1974 southern swing, but he was to appear on only one recorded cut, the title track of *Born to Run.* The selection of Max Weinberg as drummer solved what many had considered the band's roughest instrumental problem.

Keyboard player David Sancious was on the title track as well but was gone by the time Springsteen set up shop at the Record Plant. Roy Bittan was his replacement: Miami Steve Van Zandt appears only briefly on the album, but was added shortly afterward for guitar and vocal support in concert.

Bruce compared his goals on *Born to Run* as similar to those of Phil Spector or Brian Wilson in the '60s, "which is to make a *record.* To create this *sound.*"

Putting together *Born to Run* was a trying ordeal, but nothing if not memorable. All told, Bruce was in the studio for thirteen months until July 1975. "The best thing you can say about the album is that it was *the* most intense experience I ever had. There was nothing ever came close. And what was worse was, like if you can imagine being at the particular height of intensity for like *four months.* Some days when you got in there it was like murder. Some of the stuff that was in the air in that studio was *deadly.* People would *back off!*"

The "Born To Run" sessions would usually run from mid-afternoon to dawn, and sometimes go twenty-four hours nonstop. On at least one evening, things did go smoothly. On sessions for "Meeting Across the River," Landau recalls Bruce succinctly announcing "OK, I hear a string bass, and I hear a trumpet." And that was what he got, and that was what they did.

The unifying notion behind the *Born to Run* album seems simple enough, if you listen to Bruce. "The only concept that was around *Born to Run* was that I wanted to make a *big* record, you know, that sounds like these words. Just like a car, *zoom,* straight ahead, that when that sucker comes on it's like *wide open.* No holds barred!"

The album could have been called *Flight from Asbury Park;* it reflects the distance Springsteen had begun to put between himself and his old home. "I was going to have a song about back home on it, but I didn't get to it," he told Knobler. "There's a few oblique references. But most of the songs are about being *nowhere.* Just being out there in the void. Every song on the album is about that, I think. About being, like, nowhere and trying to make heads and tails out of it, you know, trying to figure it out? It's such a personal album."

"I ain't one of those guys who feels guilty if he didn't write something today," Bruce explained in *Time.* "That's all jive. If I didn't do nothing all day, I feel great."

Bruce's themes are of course taken from experience, but he does not copy day to day goings on. "You do that and this is what happens," he warns. "First you write about struggling along. Then you write about that. It's a beautiful day, you write about that. That's about twenty songs in all. Then you're out. You got nothing to write."

"The *subject* I sing about is not necessarily what I sing about. I'll use situations and probe for the very basic emotions. The conflicts I sing about are present in every level of life from the street level to the business level. With some of the newer songs I really have to dig deep inside of me to try and understand how I work so I can put it in the songs."

"The lyrics aren't as flashy now as on the first album," Bruce explained to John Rockwell. "Then it was all a lot of images. I was writing about all the things that were happening around me. If I felt right, it was okay. Lately I've been trying to deal with ideas—with concepts, with themes. The stuff I'm writin' now is closer to what I was writin' in the bars."

> "I ain't one of those guys who feels guilty if he didn't write something today . . . That's all jive. If I didn't do nothing all day, I feel great."

The *Born to Run* push began in June, when Columbia heard a rough cut of the record and used the Landau quote as the centerpiece for a campaign involving $40,000 worth of radio spots in twelve FM markets. The pieces pushed *Greetings* and *Wild and Innocent* and stressed that a third album was due soon. The first two albums more than matched their original sales as a result.

There's a poignancy to Bruce's drawling harmonics and Bittan's delicate piano as "Thunder Road" commences with the slamming of Mary's screen door and the waving of her dress in the breeze. And as Bruce the musician uses "Roy Orbison singing for the lonely" to score points with a rock audience yearning for something to bring back such glory days, Bruce the suitor uses the occasion to tell Mary that Orbison, the man from Wink, Texas, is talking about him "and I want you only."

"Thunder Road" shows a lot of the progress Bruce had made since 1973. It seems effortless enough, but this is actually a pretty complexly structured song, and I don't think Bruce could have pulled it off with the personnel on his first two albums.

"Thunder Road" gains momentum from start to finish; there are at least three places where Bruce shifts into a higher gear in his efforts to convince a reluctant Mary that "we got one last chance to make it real," and each time the band stays with him in perfect stride. A guy whose entire credo is taking action and doing stuff is finally equipped with a crew that musically knows the meaning of forward motion.

This is a song about making progress that makes progress as it goes along; the wisdom of Bruce's argument builds along with the musical crescendo. The sound is thicker and richer than before, with all five guys, Springsteen, Tallent, Weinberg, Bittan, and Clemons hanging in there together from start to glorious

finish. Along the way we get the kind of "why didn't I say that" advice that endears Bruce to his expanding audience. "Show a little faith, there's magic in the night," he assures Mary, and once again we believe it's true.

And while he berates her inclination to "waste your summer praying in vain for a saviour to rise from these streets," plenty of folks are gonna be willing to sign on and declare that he has arrived and his name is Bruce. The persuasion he uses on Mary works wonders on the listener; it's "lift yourself up by your own boot straps" dogma but that's not tough to swallow when we've got a paragon of just that which swears "it's a town full of losers and I'm pulling out of here to win." And so he does, in a flourish, with a sweeping sound of beautiful motion that is Clarence's saxophone and yes, Bittan on glockenspiel. "Thunder Road" is the most convincing argument for movin 'em out since John Wayne was in *Stagecoach*. Welcome to the bold new era of Bruce Springsteen, 1975 edition.

How he got there, how the crackerjack E Street lineup was assembled, is part of the story of "Tenth Avenue Freeze-Out." This is no musical milestone but it's a pleasant enough, good-humored tune and a step down in intensity lodged between two high-speed sequences. With a spiffy R&B arrangement aided by a guest list including the Brecker Brothers, Dave Sanborn, and Wayne Andre on horns, Bruce reviews the cold, lean times behind and the salad days that have just begun and will get even tastier. The difference came "when the change was made uptown and the Big Man joined the band" and Bruce takes no small measure of pleasure in that: "I'm gonna sit back right easy and laugh."

"Tenth Avenue Freeze-Out"

is simple and slight but a nice piece of autobiography and a breather before . . .

"Night," which begins with Max's ratatat drum burst and Clarence's reveille, is three minutes and one second of blazing energy, about folks with plenty of steam and fuel to burn after nine to five doldrums. The daily job is torture, as Bruce tells it, but "the world is busting at its seams," but you and me, the universal "you" he addresses in the song, are ready to be witnesses and active partakers.

If we argue that Bruce is egalitarian, the most democratic of pop stars, the man who cares about the young men and women who come to cheer him on, we need look no further than this track. Too often, songs sung to you, which means us, in the second person are insults; think of Billy Joel's "Captain Jack," a few doses of which could convince any hopeless suburban kid to slash his wrists. But here, Bruce puts us in the literal driver's seat, in the midst of the furious and exciting action—"Till you're out on a midnight run, losing your heart to a beautiful one, and it feels right." And there's more: "And you're in love with all the wonder it brings, and every muscle in your body sings as the highway ignites." Not only does this Springsteen fella come off his pedestal and share his world with us he *hands* it to us; it becomes our life, and life, we learn, can still be awfully good.

Our transmigration is going on while the E Street Band is just about burning out the amps; when "Night" is over, somebody better water these

guys down. These guys are not mellow; *gracias a Dios.*

Anybody who'd followed Bruce from the beginning, or at least heard his first two albums before the summer of '75, would notice one big difference here after these first three tracks. Springsteen hasn't sacrificed anything in terms of quality, creativity, or musicianship, but he's now saying what he wants in readily available, easily digestible songs. The lyrics are not nearly so complicated as they used to be, but the message is still as strong, perhaps stronger. Perhaps Bruce feels that he needn't strain his thesaurus so badly because he's now got a bunch of guys who speak very eloquently in their own tongues; the language of the drum, of the sax. The scenario of *Greetings from Asbury Park, N.J.* has been narrowed down. Now the subject is Bruce, or it's you and me, but it ain't these mysterious third persons. The scope is slimmer, but it's being viewed up close. The differences are that Bruce has learned that sometimes you can say it in three minutes, not seven, and with two characters, not twelve.

After all that is established, we move onto ' Backstreets," the magnum opus of side one. On this one, the Spectorish "wall of sound" is very much in effect. On most of *Born to Run,* the emphasis is not on individual stardom (with a few exceptions from Clarence) but on ensemble playing, on creating a collective sound much denser and fuller than the music of the first two albums. Finally he's got the personnel who can achieve that, and a lot of credit should go

to Roy Bittan. David Sancious and Danny Federici appear on the album's title track, but for the rest of the tunes it is Bittan who is brought in to handle all the keyboards. Frequently he's double-tracked on piano and organ; sometimes a third track of harpsichord or glockenspiel is added. The man's contribution is not to be overlooked; the much sought-after lushness and richness comes largely from his talented fingers.

"Backstreets" is one of the tracks that doubters have sighted in their allegation that the production of *Born to Run* is mushy, that the individual instruments cannot be heard too clearly, that Bruce's voice is sometimes lost in the mix and does not rise above it.

Such a charge ignores that the mix, used more effectively, conveys the aura of "one soft infested summer" which Bruce is singing about. This is a summer of heat, confusion, friendship, faithfulness and faithlessness; it's teeming, and producers Landau, Springsteen, and Appel (they are all credited) have successfully achieved a "teeming" sound.

I haven't counted how many times Bruce screams "hiding on the backstreets" on this track; someone wrote that there were twenty-five repetitions, but whether that is an estimate or an exact count hardly matters. What matters, and what makes the song so emotionally gripping, is that a sense of desperation and need mounts with each invocation of the backstreet muse. Here the sound and the feeling is more important than the words; Bruce lets us know that sometimes it's not so cozy being rootless and misplaced, "running for our lives at night on them backstreets." There's a universal feel to "Backstreets"; it'll move you a different way, and you'll take something else away from it each time you listen to it.

"Born to Run" opens side two, and by now there isn't

Bruce's guitar is sharp, somewhere between Duane Eddy and the Ventures; it sounds like it's accelerating on the highway. And in case we were in danger of running out of gas (and we weren't), there's a hot sax solo in which the Big Man just about launches us into the stratosphere.

Bruce's sense of comrade-

charts. Bruce might have hoped for more. "I thought I had written, like, a *classic*," he has said of the song.

Considering that the main dramatic action of "Born to Run" has Bruce asking Wendy to follow him to a loosely defined better life somewhere else, it's worth noting that at the time the album was being

> *Bruce's sense of comradeship, of togetherness, is one of his biggest drawing cards and it's heavily written into "Born to Run."*

a single person reading this book who hasn't heard it. It's got all the elements of a winner; few songs offer the listener more. At no time do we think that Bruce's "we" is limited to him and his cohort Wendy; "we" is all of us. There is ultimate escape and adventure offered here, and it's a chance not just for Wendy but for all of us. In its assurance that the bad times can be left behind, "Born to Run" rivals the Animals' "We Gotta Get Outta This Place." And in its promise that we were meant to embrace speed, chance, and danger, it matches Steppenwolf's "Born to Be Wild" stride for stride.

It's almost "wall of sound" time again, except that a couple of things stand out.

ship, of togetherness, is one of his biggest drawing cards and it's heavily written into "Born to Run." He makes his big gamble attractive and he offers us a piece of it; we all "sweat it out in the streets of a runaway American dream" and we'd love to believe that someday "we're gonna get to that place where we really want to go." For the time being, however, it is enough to remember that "tramps like us, Baby we were born to run." Especially since most of the mid-'70s rock stars only offered us the comfort of our living room. They put us into a deep spiritual coma; Bruce Springsteen snaps us out of it.

As a single, "Born to Run" made it to about number twenty on the national

made one wall of Bruce's home featured a poster of Peter Pan, guiding Wendy to Never Never Land.

There isn't a clinker on the third album, but compared to the high standards Bruce customarily offers us, "She's the One" is definitely minor. It's got a soulful early '60s sound, and when Bruce yells "hut!" the band pulls out all stops. The lore is appealing enough; he and this fancy lady would probably be better off not going near to each other— they're oil and water it would seem. But young Springsteen goes where angels fear to tread, and graciously he always takes us along. "She's the One" is good enough, but it ain't monumental. And Bruce, we've learned by now, can be monumental.

56

"Meeting Across the River" is a change of pace and interlude before the ambitious "Jungleland" finale. Except for Bittan, the E Street Band takes a rest while Bruce brings in Richard Davis on bass and Randy Brecker on trumpet.

The music here is cool, let's-bring-it-down-a-bit jazz. Sort of "it's a quarter to three, there's no one in the place except you an' me, and we're not listening too closely anyway." Bittan's fingerings are nicely meandering and Brecker sounds like he's off in the distance a bit, as if he were playing underneath the Bayonne Bridge just before dawn. Somehow it reminds me of Kirk Douglas' *Young Man with a Horn*.

Once again we find Bruce as the narrator living close to the edge. There's a tremor of terror in his voice as he asks "Hey Eddie can you lend me a few bucks?" for what sounds like a big gamble, a last chance encounter with some cats that are way out of his league. When Bruce tells Eddie "all we gotta do is hold up our end" and "tonight we got style" it doesn't sound like he believes it himself. And if this is autobiographical, Bruce lives even more dangerously than we thought. "Meeting" is a quiet piece of intrigue, showing Bruce as a master of still another style.

To some extent, "Meeting Across the River" is a harbinger of the subject matter of "Jungleland." Wild good times can get beyond control of the participants, and perhaps the stakes aren't worth it anyway. In the end, the gamblers and the chance takers can end up empty handed.

Perhaps Bruce has reached these conclusions, and has decided to leave the lifestyle and the environment behind. It's worth noting that "Jungleland" is the only track on *Born to Run* that is written in the third person. There is no expression of any notion that this is about Bruce or about us; it's about "those"

pitiful poor slobs.

If so, it's the definitive ode to the unfortunate, a final tribute if you will. "Jungleland" is a big, sprawling saga about urban night life, and if we couldn't already tell that, we'd known for sure from the Charles Calello string arrangement at the opening, which imbues the proceedings with a sense of tearful majesty.

"Jungleland" is brilliant, both in its construction and its execution. Bruce pulls us into this scene slowly, laying on details as he goes and slowly but surely getting closer to the pulse of "Jungleland."

The evening proceeds as

Bruce introduces a few chief participants, with only Bittan's piano to follow him; by now, Bittan's contribution to the *Born to Run* album seems so major that it seems a major mystery why he remains so underrated.

We learn of the Magic Rat, driving his "sleek machine" from Jersey into Manhattan, and of the barefoot girl who drinks warm beer in the rain, and of how the two of them join forces in search of romance or whatever comes first. And of the lurking Maximum Lawmen, whose mission is to make life difficult for the denizens of "Jungleland," and who do their job all too well. When he learns that all is silence "from the churches to the jails," Bittan emerges from one speaker on a very heavenly organ.

The scope of Bruce's narrative expands as "the midnight gang's assembled," and the music is likewise burgeoning as the rest of the band joins Bittan. Meeting your co-

> "Jungleland" is
> the definitive ode
> to the unfortunate
> and is brilliant in
> its construction and
> its execution.

57

horts " 'neath that giant Exxon sign that brings this fair city light" is something everyone from a town of more than 5,000 people has done, and it is now one of Bruce's signature lines.

Springsteen is one of our leading secular poets; he takes the small slice of life and gives it a grand scale. It's no surprise, then, that he doesn't just see a bunch of young folks out hustling and skirmishing; to his eyes "there's an opera out on the Turnpike, there's a ballet being fought out in the alley .

There are more images of "the hungry and the hunted," who don't particularly seem to be getting anywhere, and then a flurry of crystal clear guitar lines by Bruce, taking one of the few opportunities he takes on the album to show that he sure can play. The guitar solo serves as a transition to an even more heated picture of lovers struggling, backstreet girls dancing and a desperate night that dissolves into Clarence Clemons on the saxophone.

Clarence's solo is a kind of signal to regroup, rethink, and cool down. The Big Man doesn't dazzle with anything fancy here but he bridges the gap beautifully between the night's frenzy and its aftermath. It's as if a thundering wave is coming in with Clarence at its crest, and he rides it from its breaking point to its slow drift back out to sea. When the wave's busted he hands things back to Bruce, who surveys the carnage and picks up the pieces for us.

It is not a pretty picture. Among other things, the Magic Rat's dream has been shot to pieces, and so has he;

an ambulance carts him away. Nothing seems to be working out; nobody seems to be getting anywhere. Finally, Springsteen makes his pronouncement:

RICHARD McCAFFREE

*Outside the street's on fire
In a real death waltz
Between what's flesh and
    what's fantasy
And the poets down here
Don't write nothing at all
They just stand back and
    let it all be.*

They "reach for their moment," but it is for naught. They "wind up wounded, not even dead." Somehow it sounds so much worse.

What's so striking about this climactic section of "Jungleland" is how disapproving Springsteen is; it's one of the rare times that he's judgemental and doesn't leave the deciding to us.

"The poets down here don't write nothing at all" is sung

58

in a fit of anger as if it is the worst condemnation possible. To Bruce, it may well be. In subsequent interviews, he has indicted fears about talent that could go to waste [his] much more than actual words and for which he is justly famed. It's a real emotional outburst, with Bittan's piano accompaniment scurrying like a madman beneath it. "Jun- does with anything negative. It is as if Bruce is telling us that after much reflection, he is undergoing a painful withdrawal from the world he has documented on the rest of

RICHARD McCAFFREE

and lamented about gifts that have already been squandered [these other 'poets.''].

The conclusion of "Jungleland" is a passage of pure anguish for Springsteen—cries of pain, the kind of "whoaoahs" and "hoo-oos" which say so gleland" is a spasm of pain, a wail of the unfulfilled.

It is lengthy, complex, troublesome, and totally effective. It is a song of suffering on an album that deals far more with joy or at the very least with hope, than it *Born to Run*. He couldn't have known what lay ahead, but in many ways "Jungleland" is a prophetic glimpse at some of the hardships that lay ahead before he could ever complete his follow-up album.

Born to Run deserved its

> *When* <u>Born to Run</u> *was completed, Bruce "hated it. I couldn't stand to listen to it. I thought it was the worst piece of garbage I'd ever heard."*

rise to number one and platinum status. It has something for everyone who wants to listen. There are formidable epics of the grand scale ("Backstreets" and "Jungleland"), some readily accessible pop tunes ("She's the One" and "Tenth Avenue Freeze-Out") and a few anthems of the age, words and music to live by ("Thunder Road," "Night," and "Born to Run"). Most importantly Springsteen gave us the sounds we wanted to hear, returned to us the energy we'd been missing, and involved *us* in his oeuvre to an extent that no other rocker before or since has done.

Knobler noted of *Born to Run,* "the stuff that stole us away from our parents is there and more."

Yet it wasn't an immediate hit with everyone. In San Mateo, where she was living with her parents, Bruce's thirteen-year-old sister Pam noted that only one girl in her school had a copy of *Born to Run.*

It may have been the psychological let down of having finally completed what was beginning to seem like a life's work, or maybe it's just that Bruce's critical capabilities are not nearly a match for his creative ones, but when *Born to Run* was completed he "hated it. I couldn't stand to listen to it. I thought it was the worst piece of garbage I'd ever heard. I told Columbia I wouldn't release it. I told 'em I'd just go down to the Bottom Line gig and do all the new songs and make it a live album." Fortunately, record companies do occasionally know how to say no to their artists.

In *Playboy* Springsteen explained, "working on *Born to Run* was a very scary thing. I was born, grew old and died making that album. We knew what we wanted to do; it was just a very hard thing to do. We weren't making mistakes. The E Street Band doesn't make mistakes."

"*Born to Run* seems one of the great records of recent years," John Rockwell declared in the *New York Times.* Rockwell believed Bruce was "a man who just might be the next Mr. Jagger." (In the *Times,* every male over sixteen is called mister.)

In the *Village Voice,* Paul Nelson called Springsteen "the only artist I know who could combine the sound of Phil Spector with the singing of Roy Orbison" and noted of the live shows "Springsteen fashions the kind of seamless, 150-minute performance that most artists only dream about."

There were some folks, people who'd followed Bruce from his early and obscure days, who didn't really approve of the direction taken on *Born to Run* and felt, like Joe Edwards of New Jersey's *Aquarian* that it was his "weakest album to date."

Edwards, who believed the title track was "easily the best rock and roll song of the year and perhaps the decade" and also praised "Thunder Road" and "Backstreets," felt the rest of the album was "mostly formulaic derivative, clumsily written" and that the Spectorish wall of sound "renders almost every song as muddy and incoherent and non-musical as anything on the Rolling Stones' *Exile on Main Street.*

The *Aquarian* writer, who maintained his faith that Springsteen is "one of the best we have " said that for listeners like himself who "prefer crispness, who like to hear what the individual musicians are doing, who get off on fine lyrics—especially Springsteen's song poems—this album's production will be an insurmountable object blocking the way to enjoyment."

Landon Winner, in a mixed review in the *Real Paper*, subscribed to the view that the jury was still out on Bruce's ability to become the Great White Hope rock so obviously needed. "He could be of the Olivia Newton-Johns and the likes of the Carpenters."

Richard Meltzer, one of the first serious rock critics, said after seeing Bruce at the Bottom Line, "he's not as good a singer as Peter Wolf (J. Geils Band), and he can't move as good as Iggy. He's just what the public is ready to accept commercially—like Elton John. He's not even as good as Dion."

has portrayed his native Asbury Park as both a heavenly and a hellish city," Holden commented, "his *Born to Run* fixes it in hell for sure." The writer said Bruce's singing on songs like "Jungleland" and "Backstreets" featured "feral howls and moans of agonized despair whose intensity is bonechilling.

"Springsteen reminds us that rock & roll came from the streets as a cultural neces-

> ## "I told Columbia I wouldn't release it. I told 'em I'd just go down to the Bottom Line gig and do all the new songs and make it a live album."

music's next Rocky Marciano," noted Winner. "Then again he could be our next Duane Bobick."

The word from Bruce's old local rag, the *Asbury Park Press,* was generally favorable but tempered a bit. Staff writer Marty Packin observed "as lyricist and studio performer, Jackson Browne outweighs him by a great deal. The same goes for the Walter Becker/Donald Fagen song writing team and the sound of their Steely Dan."

Yet Packin conceded a point which may have been the reason why Bruce's popularity quickly became so widespread. "He certainly outshines a musical scene made up

But Andy Shernoff of the New York band The Dictators (who were later to befriend Bruce) believed "he has the best show in America —even better than Kiss. He's much more human."

Nick Cohn, in *New York,* explained how he felt many people were drawn to Springsteen despite their better judgement. "He is peddling a vision—mock-tragic runts on the skids—that I have always found irrestible, and though I know that I am being duped, the fraud still excites me, I cannot muster resentment."

Stephen Holden in *Circus Raves* saw *Born to Run* as a darker shade of Springsteen. "If, in the past, Springsteen

sity, an instinctual urge toward self-transcendance and self-definition," Holden observed. "I've no doubt that rock & roll has literally saved Bruce Springsteen from the mute tragedy of life in a 'Jungle-land.'"

Greil Marcus, the only rock critic ever nominated for a National Book Award, observed in *Rolling Stone,* "Springsteen's singing, his words, and the band's music have turned the dreams and failures two generations have dropped along the road into an epic—an epic that began when that car went over the cliff in *Rebel Without A Cause.*"

Marcus noted, "the songs

> *"The only artist I know who could combine the sound of Phil Spector with the singing of Roy Orbison."*

can, as with 'Backstreets,' hit so hard and fast that it is almost impossible to sit through them without weeping. And yet the music is exhilarating. You may find yourself shaking your head in wonder, smiling through tears at the beauty of it all. I'm not talking about lyrics; they're buried, as they should be, hard to hear for the first dozen playings or so, coming out in bits and pieces. To hear Springsteen sing the line 'Hiding on the backstreets' is to be captured by an image; the details can come later."

Bruce probably wouldn't make the comment now, since the current E Street line-up seems just about ideal, but in 1974, when the band was still going through a revolving door, he said in a *Sounds* interview, "the band's built to be flexible. That way if everybody leaves tomorrow or everybody stays it'll work out. You can get mediocre guys and if you have the right arrangements and know what to do with them you'll still have a good band."

With the release of *Born to Run* and the subsequent long and celebrated 1975 concert tour, the reputation of the E Street Band was solidified. Dave March was to call them

"one of the finest rock and roll groups ever assembled," and *Time* was later to declare, "they are powerhouse musicians who have raised roadhouse rock to Olympian heights."

Bearded bassist Garry Tallent was with Bruce in Dr. Zoom and the Sonic Boom in 1971. In the great E Street tradition, he owns a 1948 Rock Ola jukebox and 3,000 oldies (probably more by now). Tallent is known to be extremely partial to "rockabilly" music and must have been thrilled in '78 when Springsteen, after seeing *The Buddy Holly Story*, added "Rave On" to the live shows.

Tallent went to the same New Jersey high school as Jack Nicholson—Neptune High School—and once, at the height of Springsteen mania, spent three hours in a Los Angeles bar with Nicholson bemoaning the fact that the entire world seemed to hail from New Jersey.

Tallent and Springsteen first met in a Jersey shore club where Garry apparently stared Bruce off the stage and persuaded the Boss to come hear him play. Tallent, sometimes called Funk, says he broke down and cried the first time he heard Roy Orbi-

son's "Running Scared" on the car radio. That was all the recommendation Springsteen needed.

Of the early, formative music making days with Bruce, Garry told Richard Price in *Playboy*, "a bunch of us used to get together at a club called the Upstage and jam for two hours on 'I'm a Man'. We formed bands. We always thought Bruce was a good act. If there was a chance of any of us making a living through music, we figured it would have to happen through him."

Roy Bittan is always dubbed "The Professor" these days. He's named for Professor Longhair, the sixty-year-old barrel-house and blues pianist whose most recent album was a recorded concert at a party given by Paul McCartney on the Queen Mary in Long Beach. Bittan joined the E Street Band after passing an audition which had been advertised in a newspaper. Within a short time, he would be challenging Clarence as the most important instrumentalist backing Bruce. Bittan is the only band member not from New Jersey; he hails from Rockaway Beach in Queens.

Bittan replaced David Sanci-

ous in September of 1974. Sancious was an excellent and versatile musician with some classical and jazz leanings who had even done string arrangements on *The Wild, the Innocent, and the E Street Shuffle.* Gradually, his presence may have become an issue of compatibility. He obviously had his own muse to follow. After a stint with jazz bassist Stanley Clarke, Sancious went on to form his own band, Tone, which is signed to Arista Records and features Ernest "Boom" Carter on drums.

Drummer Max Weinberg is never known as anything but Mighty Max, and correctly so; he is an astonishingly powerful, rapid fire percussionist. Mighty Max has alleviated what was generally considered to be the E Street Band's biggest manpower problem, and he arrived in the most democratic fashion; he won the job in audition. His previous credits included time spent in the Broadway pit orchestras of *Godspell* and *The Magic Show.*

Weinberg is thrilled to be a part of the E Street gang, and his faith in the Boss is complete. In *Gallery,* he told Paul Williams, "it's a very professional scene. He [Bruce] knows what he wants and what he's doing. He's the ideal bandleader—he makes you want to play, want to create. The band works off Bruce. There's a tremendous energy on stage, and it's all of us but it's directed by one person.

"I've never enjoyed anything so much in my life " Weinberg told Williams. "Everybody in this band has got his act together. People say, 'It looks like you guys are really having fun out there'. We are

I am. Nobody's doing a number on anybody else's head. On the road it works like a machine. It's beautiful."

Sandy-haired Danny Federici is a long-time Springsteen colleague who was a member of Steel Mill and of the later ten-piece group with girl singers that Bruce fronted. On record and on stage, he primarily plays organ, but his virtuosity as an accordionist gives the E Street Band an unusual extra instrumental option.

Bruce has not only been Federici's bandleader; he's been his baby sitter. Danny's ex-wife Florence told a New Jersey newspaperman in '75 about the house Springsteen shared with the Federicis and other friends in Bradley Beach in the winter of 1970. To her, Springsteen seemed to be primarily a loner, but when he would sit for the Federicis' infant son, he'd play his guitar for the baby, who was reportedly one of his earliest fans.

Bruce's long-time friend Miami Steve Van Zandt, who'd played only a small role in the recording of *Born to Run,* was added to the concert lineup as a guitarist and harmony singer. As we will observe later, Steve's role in the E Street Band would grow considerably over the years.

And there is Clarence Clemons, immortalized on the famous Eric Meola cover of *Born to Run,* a titanic presence and saxophonist extraordinaire who has become a celebrity in his own right and almost as much a part of the E Street legend as the Boss himself.

Springsteen totally understands the value both musi-

cally and imagewise of Clarence and reserves a special introduction for him on the concert stage. He presents Clarence to the assembled multitudes as:

"The King of the World,
The Master of the Universe,
More Powerful Than a Locomotive,
Able to Leap Tall Refineries in a Single Bound,
It's a Bird, It's a Plane,
It's the Big Man on the Saxophone!"

Clarence is originally from Norfolk, Virginia, but came to the northern New Jersey area in the mid-'60s. He is every bit the "Big Man" he has been affectionately dubbed by Springsteen. A one-time teacher in a reform school, he was a football line backer for the minor league Newark Bears and set for the big time with the Cleveland Browns when injuries in an auto accident curtailed his gridiron career.

His first meeting with the Boss used to make for an intriguing stage rap; Bruce would talk about how this big black dude had just come trucking around the corner, with his huge shiny tenor saxophone in hand. Occasionally, Bruce would add that he was huddled under an arcade, shivering and seeking shelter from a hurricane, when the unperturbed Clarence walked by.

Whatever the weather, the historic meeting took place, says Clarence, "through a mutual friend while we were walkin' down the boardwalk one night. Bruce was playing in a bar band and we got to jamming. Before that, I didn't know who he was or anything."

No band leader could ever ask for a stronger virtuoso or charismatic presence for a first mate than Clarence Clemons, but the Big Man keeps it clear that "Bruce definitely calls all the shots. And he's actually an inspiration for all of us in the band. I guess you could say it's Bruce Springsteen and band, not just the Bruce Springsteen Band."

Springsteen impressed Clemons as being someone extraordinary from the very beginning. "I guess the first thing you notice about him is the force of energy he has," he told Philadelphia journalist David Fricke. "It's in every-

thing he does. It's real. A real energy."

Clarence, who spent some time with James Brown and the Fabulous Flames, marvels, "it's amazing the control Bruce has, especially over an audience. Like instinct—he knows what the audience wants and just how to give it to them."

One thing Bruce gives them is choreography involving Clarence, a kind of bump and grind bit in which they trade licks. They lean on each other, as on the *Born to Run* cover. Or they may even chase each other around the stage.

"Nothing is really rehearsed," notes Clarence. "It just comes off the energy of the moment.

You watch it happen each night on stage. With all that energy, you want to do it."

He continues, "I guess you could call it a communication between the two of us. Almost like intuition. The whole band, too—I have never been in a band where people respect him so much. He's in control of the whole scene." And the whole band gels together. "We all kinda think alike—just from working together for so long," says the sax man.

Clarence picked up the sax at age nine. His direction has always been fairly clear; he's not a jazzman. "Yeah, I dig people like Junior Walker and King Curtis," he told Fricke.

"Lately, I've been getting into Gato Barbieri, a real energy player. You see, the tenor sax is a power horn. I'm not so into Coltrane. He's more of a free-form jazz thing. I'm more r&b. You can just call me a rock player. I play rock 'n' roll sax."

There have always been whispers about how the E Street gang, anxious to get the product before the people, get more than a little edgy sitting around in the studio while their perfectionist boss keeps declaring "no, that's not right."

There is, however, always pressure on Bruce to live up to his promise, to deliver a product that is not just good but truly remarkable, even trail blazing in the rock field. Some of the pressure was real, some of it brought on himself by Bruce, by his very nature.

Such pressure was particularly intense during the making of *Born to Run,* seen by many as the album that was going to make or break Springsteen's career in the commercial sense.

It was a period made even more difficult by the personnel changes the band was undergoing; Bittan and Weinberg had just come in to replace David Sancious and Vini "Mad Dog" Lopex. A trying time for sure, but Clarence, for one, did not lose faith.

"I was kind of patient," he recalls. "Bruce knew what he was doing and we all knew it. And besides, as long as we're out there playing, it's all right. Sure, it got tense, laying around waiting for it to happen. But I knew everything was gonna work out."

When the album was finally released, Clarence, like just about everyone, was a bit stunned by the concurrent media madness, but it was by no means a complete surprise. "I expected it all the time, even when I first met Bruce,"

he observes. "When you see someone put out that much energy, energy that's real, you know it's gonna come out sooner or later. It was just a long time comin'."

Philosophically, Clemons commented "all of a sudden,

everybody's saying how we're an overnight success and all that. But we've been doing the same thing for years. People are just becoming aware of it, that's all. Sometimes when people come up to us and say about how we're an overnight success, I felt like asking 'em, 'where the hell you been all this time?'"

For the present, Clarence, a star in his own right, is one contented Big Man. "My whole goal in life is to be happy," he states. "I just want to dig what I'm doing. And right now I dig what I'm doing with Bruce. All the way."

Bruce has said of the Big Man, "Clarence and I are like that," crossing his fingers tightly. "His music and my music are ideally suited. We breathe the same thing."

"Clarence is his sax," Springsteen believes. "Sometimes you can't tell where Clarence ends and his sax begins." And while the Big Man is quite a hulking presence, the Boss promises "ah, he's a pussycat."

For Clarence, no stage manager is necessary; the directions are quite elementary. "You hook on to Bruce on that stage and you go wherever he takes you," the Big Man says. "It's like total surrender to him."

In Bruce's "dream band," the E Street lineup of the moment, "every guy in the band hits the right note. Not any note, but the *right* note. If you like rock and roll, you gotta like our band. The guys have got a great sense of history about them. We're a real American band; there are practically no European influences."

Springsteen said in a *Playboy* article, "those guys are so good they're down to intangibles. At the Bottom Line, I climbed out across the tables, into the audience, and looked at those guys just standing there on stage doing their stuff. I almost didn't come back. We play the same notes every night, but sometimes something happens. Maybe it's a guy's face in the front row. Maybe it's something someone says. But it happens and it's what we play for. Some bands something starts happening on stage, they fuck up. Not my guys."

Unfortunately, Springsteen believes that this wonderfulness does not translate in the studio. "It's a different thing. You get by on your ability to do the same thing twenty-five times in a row. It's not creative. You are what you know, what you've learned. It's almost impossible to get a spark going, 'cause that spark doesn't come from technique."

Robert Ward of *New Times* called the E Street Band a group that "can drop the bottom out and pick it back up without missing so much as a sixteenth of a note." The very real and genuine rush of seeing Springsteen and his cronies perform was to Ward "not unlike seeing the high school girl of your dreams divorced and still aching for you at some sleazy bar."

Paul Williams considered Bruce and the E Street Band "the best live rock group of the 1970s so far" and marveled "they put out so much excitement in their stage show, wherever they play, that I'd go to their concerts even if I were deaf—just to watch."

The Bottom Line engagement, coming in August just on the heels of the *Born to Run* release, was Bruce's most important engagement as far as impressing the people in the music business itself was concerned. All manner of radio, record company, and rock press persons were crowded into the tiny Village venue to see if this Springsteen fellow was everything he was cracked up to be.

Dave Herman, the early morning deejay on WNEW-FM, New York's most influential progressive station, saw one of The Bottom Line shows and was converted. Herman hadn't even played *Greetings from Asbury Park, N.J.* on the air. "The Dylan hype from Columbia was a turnoff. I didn't even bother to listen to it. I didn't want Columbia to think they got me."

But after seeing Bruce live, Herman made what amounted to an on-air apology. "I saw Springsteen for the first time last night," he told his listeners. "It's the most exciting rock 'n' roll show I've ever seen."

After witnessing The Bottom Line engagement, Mitchell Cohen, writing in *Good Times,* stated "Bruce Springsteen's success is a blow for quality rock and roll, a victory for music that has both imagery and energy."

Record World, a publication for industry insiders, lauded Springsteen for winning over a throng that "consisted mostly of rock critics and music industryites, not the easiest crowd to conquer." But their writer, Mike Sigman, worried that the high-powered, insistant performance by the Boss might be too much for the audience to keep up with.

"The required level of concentration could not be sustained by the audience for over two hours without some kind of relief," said the weary writer.

The title of Kenneth Tucker's *Soho Weekly News* review saluted Bruce's "sublime excessiveness," and Tucker's enthusiasm was not understated. "I have just come from the best rock & roll performance I've ever seen in my long, decadent life," marvelled the critic who agreed "Springsteen may well be the saviour of rock & roll that many assert he is."

Tucker's comments weren't 100 percent favorable; he contended "Springsteen is no great genius at lyric-writing . . . his words and stories are no more profound than Jan and Dean's." There's certainly plenty of room for disagreement there, but Tucker tempers his comments with an astute observation: "since at his best Springsteen is loud and manic, lyrics are of lesser importance, and New York Romanticism is a ready-made framework from which to extract *anything* that fits metrically into one of his brilliant melodies." Tucker concluded with the bold comment "Springsteen is a better scat-singer than Van Morrison and Joe Cocker combined."

The most cogent review of The Bottom Line dates probably came from Bruce himself. "The band cruised through them shows like the finest machine there was. There's nothin'—nothin'—in the world to get you playing better than a gig like that," he said afterward. "The band walked out of The Bottom Line twice as good as when

69

CHUCK PULIN

they walked in." It was a true baptism of fire and he'd walked through it shining.

Bruce's hour in the spotlight seemed to have come. He seemed tailor made for the times.

As Alan Betrock wrote in 1975, "the public has been without a real hero for years, now, an individual who can inspire and reenergize initiative, rather than gaze down from atop a perch offering little more than frivolous, vain, and self-serving pronouncements."

New Times writer Robert Ward saw Springsteen as a man who "just radiates energy, and soul. And unlike Jagger, Springsteen is not aloof, not aristocratic. He's the ultimate Good Punk."

Indeed, one of the most magical factors about Bruce Springsteen is that he may be the least plutocratic of rock idols. He knows that but for the grace of God or whatever he would be out there in the chairs, not up on stage. Ward commented "there is a minimum of distance between Springsteen and the audience. He's a star and he's a vamp, but he's got a wonderful sense of pure joy in his playing, which is immediately identifiable as democratic. His persona *is* punky, but there is an intelligence behind it that says, 'Hey, this is just good old rock and roll and let's get it on'. In short, he's having too much fun to be pompous."

Bruce was residing in Atlantic Highlands, N.J. in 1975, so it was easy enough for him to return home for two sold-out shows at the Carlton Theater in Red Bank, in the shadow of Asbury Park, just two weeks before he was on the cover of *Time* and *Newsweek*.

The marquee read "Homecoming '75" for the return of Monmouth County's most famous native son. Many of the people in the audience remembered Bruce and many of the E Street lads from as far back as five or six years ago, when they were shuffling at clubs like Pandemonium in Wanamassa and the Student Prince and the Upstage in Asbury Park.

They remembered him as the Freehold High School kid whose 1967 yearbook picture on page 71 showed a clean-shaven face and not a single extracurricular activity. They remembered him as one acquaintance described him: "a dude who couldn't do anything else. Hell, he couldn't even drive a car until he was 19."

On stage at the Carlton, Bruce swore, "there's no place like home," apparently meaning it in a positive sense for the moment. When he introduced the Manfred Mann song "Pretty Flamingo" (the Mann group's singer Paul Jones is one of his vocal idols) Bruce recalled his adolescence in the area.

"I wanna dedicate this song to all the girls," he began. "Cause this is a song about the kind of girl you can't go up to talk to. Man, I couldn't talk to girls at all. Me and Steve used to sit on my front porch when I lived on South Street in Freehold. Every day at 5:00 this girl would walk by and I wanted to go up and talk to her.

"I'd say to Steve 'Go talk to her, man'. And we'd sit there like two fools. We tried to get the crazy kid on the block to do it for us." Bruce and Steve would wonder what her name was. Finally, they called her "Pretty Flamingo."

From other examples of his concert reminiscences about his younger days, it seems that Bruce, Steve, and their buddies spent a lot of time on front porches and board-walks trying to figure out how to talk to girls.

The return of the prodigal Bruce to Monmouth County led to local newspaper interviews with folks who had known Bruce "when." Carl "Tinker" West, owner of a surfboard factory in Ocean Township, let Bruce live upstairs over the factory in 1970, and in that same year drove Springsteen to California for a gig that paid $2,200. It was on that epic journey that Bruce learned how to drive. It was also West who nicknamed Bruce the Gut Bomb King in honor of his penchant for fast foods.

The job to which Tinker drove Bruce was a New Year's Eve show at the Esalen Institute. "I've never been outta Jersey in my life and suddenly I get to Esalen and see all these people walkin' around in sheets," Bruce said

One of the most magical factors about Bruce Springsteen is that he may be the least plutocratic of rock idols. He knows that but for the grace of God or whatever he would be out there in the chairs, not up on stage.

71

of it later. "I see someone playing bongos in the woods and it turns out to be this guy who grew up around the corner from me." Alas, Bruce did not return a superstar. "Nobody wanted to listen to a guy with a guitar," he sighed.

His second grade teacher at St. Rose Grammar School in Freehold remembers having to constantly reprimand him for daydreaming. A former classmate recalls that Bruce walked down the street with his head down, and seemed tired all the time.

A high school music teacher remembers the future musical sensation would just sit in the back of the room, saying nothing. Some folks remembered every one of his fledgling bands, from Castile to Child to Steel Mill to Dr. Zoom and the Sonic Boom. The Castiles were formed during Bruce's sophomore year, and Bruce's first playing gigs were CYO dances at St. Rose Church in Freehold.

The interviews also uncovered the reasons why the E Street gang's Monopoly games always featured a special Chief McCarthy card, which sent the bearer to jail for no reason. It seemed that McCarthy was a local police chief who broke up a successful Steel Mill gig in the town of Highlands in September, 1970. Bruce and his band had attracted 3,000 fans to a place called the Clearwater Swim Club, and McCarthy and his boys tried to halt the performance at 10 p.m. What resulted were injuries to police and spectators and charges of harassment and police brutality, well-documented in the local press.

Newark Star-Ledger columnist George Kanzler, Jr., understood how much Bruce meant to the Jersey kids. "He's invested their commonplace lives their little Saturday night adventures, their teen rituals and reckless highways moments with all the significance of rock and roll myth," Kanzler conjectured. "He's not the only hero, they are too. Springsteen, with his music, has done more than any Chamber of Commerce or tourist promoter could do. He's made the Jersey Shore musically important, nationally."

Springsteenmania was not confined to New York and New Jersey. Four shows at Philadelphia's Tower Theater, 12,000 tickets in all, sold out in ninety minutes, and one columnist reported "some sickos are breaking into homes to steal Springsteen tickets." In Lenox, Massachusetts, Springsteen obliged a crowd of 5,000 (7,000 had been turned away) with three encores, but the crowd was still hollering half an hour later, even though the stage crew was dismantling Bruce's equipment.

Bruce was also selling out houses in Austin, Houston, and New Orleans, although Dallas greeted him with a half-empty house at the Convention Center. In New Orleans, Bruce completed two encores and the lights went up, but Louisianans weren't about to let him escape. Finally Bruce came back, dragging Boz Scaggs from backstage, and the two teamed up for "Twist and Shout."

Everyone wanted to touch a little of the Springsteen magic. While in Chicago, Bruce and the boys were invited to take a tour of America's most famed pleasure "hutch," the Playboy Mansion, and they obliged. Soon, however, they were off in the night for their brand of activity—a dinner of pizza and a trip to the Queen Bee Club on the South Side to see bluesman Junior Wells.

The California reception to Bruce was mixed. San Francisco was a sellout, but the 4,000-seat Memorial Auditorium in Sacramento was one-third empty. But he was a big hit in Santa Monica. "I've never seen such control," a Columbia staffer said after seeing that Springsteen show "He'd take two steps back and stare at one group in the audience, and they'd immediately leap to their feet."

Bruce's fans are among the most rabid concert goers; they come close to frothing at the mouth.

"Last week there was a rowdy crowd: man, those dudes were ROWDY out there for the first act and I had to come out and cool them out for this dude that was ahead of me," Springsteen mentioned about a '75 gig. "I came out and I said, 'Listen, lighten up on this poor guy. Give him a break, give *me* a break, this is embarrassing to me' and rah rah, y'know. We came out, and the audience was a lamb for the whole set. It was so quiet it was unbelievable. Yet they blasted this guy offstage which was a drag because he was good.

"See, I'm not into people screaming at me, like Bowie," Bruce explained. "Once they do that, it's over. I'll go back to playing the small clubs. I'm not there for them any-

Hollywood debut at the Roxy, 1975

way. I'm there for me, y'know, that's all. If they can dig it, cool, if not, they don't have to come. I'll still be the same. A lot of times the audience thinks they are there to scream at you. They think that's what you want, maybe. And that's not it. I can dig silence after a tune. Like, we did 'I Want You' and the response was not exactly, well, it was somewhat confused. Some were digging it and others weren't sure. I can dig that, that got me off.''

In that other rock capital on the opposite coast, Los Angeles, Bruce was booked for an important meeting with the media at the Roxy. Among the West Coast Springsteen buffs were Flo and Eddie, who postponed a booking in the same city rather than compete with Bruce.

They added, ''We'd rather see Bruce than play ourselves.''

The starstudded Roxy crowd included Jack Nicholson, Tatum O'Neal and her father Ryan, Neil Diamond, Wolfman Jack, and assorted Carpenters, Beatles, and Beach Boys.

Stan Findelle, discussing the Roxy shows in *Performance*, the international talent weekly, contended ''as 1975 fades to a close it has become increasingly obvious that the music industry is still desperately searching for a great white hope, someone who personifies a radical yet consumable digression so necessary for the aesthetic, as well as guy who somehow got the covers of *Time* and *Newsweek* on the same date. It was October 27, 1975, while the E Street entourage was still in Los Angeles. The distinction, for a relative unknown, mystified some. street. They only hear the music. If they like it, they buy it. And if they don't, no cover pictures on any magazine in the world can make them buy it."

Still, people wanted to know the answer to the question

> ## "There is a danger I could be treated like a product instead of a person."

economic perpetuation of the rock genre. It seems now that Bruce Springsteen, whether justified or not, has been enlisted to play the role."

Findelle felt Springsteen arrived in Los Angeles "draped in the purple robes of hyperbole for a carnival of contrivance," replete with enough movie stars in the audience to seem "like a scene being shot on a motion picture soundstage."

Amidst the hoopla, Findelle remained unimpressed. "If he could only just play rock—instead of roles," yearned the writer. "There is nothing about him such that he could be called 'an original'. His costumed posture of patent punk and leather has little more credibility than when Sha Na Na uses it. How many times must we revisit Highway 61?"

To many people who know nothing about him, who have never heard his records or seen his concerts, Bruce Springsteen is identifiable as that

But Bruce and his buddies knew what to expect. During the week of the Roxy engagement, Miami Steve commented, "we're due for a vacation. Bruce's time is totally accounted for with the morning interview, the afternoon interview. Now it's gonna get worse with these two stories. Everybody's gonna be asking what it's like to be a phenomenon. I don't even know how to spell the word. Is that with a P or an F? There are journalists hanging around our home town interviewing our friends, record scouts hunting for the Asbury Park sound. We gotta live there, too, you know."

"There is a danger I could be treated like a product instead of a person. I have to be careful," a prophetic Bruce told British journalist Bob Hart after the Roxy dates. "A lot of things are being said about me, and some of them are crazy. But none of those things affects the kids in the

Chicago Sun-Times columnist Bob Greene asked immediately. "How in hell does a semi-unknown kid who isn't even a real star get his face on the cover of *Time* and *Newsweek* simultaneously?"

Newsweek tried to give its own answer the following week. In their words, "*Newsweek* began working three weeks ago on an article about Springsteen as the most exciting new rock personality in several years. Probably for similar reasons, *Time*, a few days later, began working on a Springsteen cover of its own."

They even interviewed the competition. *Time* managing editor Henry Grunwald explained, "you can't edit a magazine trying to avoid what someone else may or may not be doing."

The article also noted Bruce's own wry comment on the matter. "Why should I be on the cover of *Newsweek*?" he wanted to know. "I don't deserve it. That's for Presidents."

In fact, it was in *Newsweek* that Bruce tried to put the whole hype question into perspective. "We're driving around, and we ain't no phenomenon," he explained. "The hype just gets in the way. People have gone nuts. It's weird. All the stuff you dream about is there, but it gets diluted by all the other stuff that jumped on you by surprise."

And in *Time* he commented, "I don't understand what all the commotion is about. I feel like I'm on the outside of all this, even though I know I'm on the inside. It's like you want attention, but sometimes you can't relate to it."

In recognition of his media stardom, Springsteen now changes a key line in "Rosalita" to "cause I got my picture on the cover of *Time* and *Newsweek*."

Interestingly, Mike Appel had actually rejected a *Newsweek* request for an interview back in September, as he held out for a cover or nothing at all. "That was a pretty bold step at the time," one Columbia publicist observed. Appel, in 1975, asked for circulation audits of papers wanting interviews.

Bruce became such a press phenomenon that even *Vogue* had something to say about him. E Street punk had become chic in November of '75. They observed; "He's sweet and sexy and makes you laugh . . . He's fabulous! He kicks his feet in the air and saunters about the stage with sass . . . He's one of the most seductive and talented singers to come along since Dylan! He soulfully rasps and grumbles

and whispers his songs—backed by his incredible E Street Band. Watch for his new album, *Born to Run*. Sensational."

One of the more bizarre, unexpected, and perhaps a bit farfetched reactions to the Springsteen case came from someone who usually commented on more weighty affairs—Martin Nolan, the political columnist and Washington Bureau chief of the *Boston Globe*. The Springsteen push and the race for the 1976 presidential nominations were both heating up in December of 1975, and Nolan saw parallels between Bruce and, of all people, Ronald Reagan.

"Ronald Reagan may be the Bruce Springsteen of politics. And Bruce Springsteen may be the Ronald Reagan of rock," he observed. "Rock fans and Republican voters both swoon over the familiar; both demand an echo, not a choice."

The much respected Nolan, who may have been trying to expand his reading constituency, believed "Springsteen evokes Bob Dylan as faithfully as Reagan recalls Barry Goldwater. Both, therefore, are prominent in the current media market of recycled, hyped-up nostalgia."

Nolan, making his first bid at rock criticism, said of Bruce, "his voice is even weaker than Dylan's and his incessant whine is made even more discordant by indifferent melodies and unmetrical lyrics." He suggested that both Springsteen and Reagan, who also appeared on *Time* and *Newsweek* covers in the same week, were getting near the top without answering hard, specific questions. Nolan

concludes, "both were born to run."

With so much effusive media mania about Bruce the Wonder Boy flooding the airways and newsstands in 1975, it remained for some foul-hearted demon to deflate the *Born to Run* balloon. He was called Henry Edwards, and he was later to earn dubious credit for writing the screenplay for *Sgt. Pepper's Lonely Heart's Club Band*. In the midst of the Springsteen hoopla, Edwards, in a long *New York Times* article, observed in his title "If There Hadn't Been a Bruce Springsteen, Then the Critics Would Have Made Him Up."

The naysaying Edwards wanted to know, "what about the conspicuous flaws in his music making? Why have most critics ignored these flaws?"

Edwards saw Bruce as a B-film stereotype, the outlaw teen who is "lonely, lost, and desperate, and his only release is to toss a girl into a car and zoom down a highway to nowhere."

To Edwards' ear, the musical accompaniment on *Born to Run* was "simply torrential" and overwhelmed Bruce's baritone; in concert the band offered up "sledgehammer blows" suitable only for someone who "exults in pounding repetition."

He considered the album's Springsteen-Appel-Landau production to be responsible for "musical sludge" and that Springsteen was "virtually burrowing his way out of the bottom of a musical tunnel of his own devising."

Edwards questioned Springsteen's originality, believing he "simply pastes together

75

> *No one understands better than Bruce that music could be a form of deliverance.*

bits and pieces, and many of the bits thus embalmed are copies of some of rock 'n' roll's finest moments." "She's the One" sounded to him like TV's "Shindig" theme, and "Born to Run" had an intro copped from the Raspberries and a midsection straight out of Alice Cooper.

The writer, viewing the new media favorite on stage, observed "never at rest, he swaggers, whirls, kicks, leaps, pirouettes, jumps onto the piano and occasionally improvises a dance that looks like a madcap tango. Eventually, his movements become as repetitious as his lyrics."

Edwards' commentary was not without some astute points about the climate of the music business in 1975 Of the record company execs so heavily pushing Springsteen he said "their business depends on the creation of new sensations every year. Accordingly, they have to promote *somebody.*

He conjectured that Springsteen must have observed that "in this time of record industry doldrums, the return of the middle-of-the-road performers such as Paul Anka and the popularity of disco music, there is a large potential rock music audience which feels neglected. In such

a climate, the very derivativeness of Springsteen's music, and the throw-back quality of his punkish persona have an irresistible appeal "to young fans creating new heroes and older ones nostalgic for the days when rock stars were viewed as rebels or a 'challenge to the establishment.' "

None of this, Edwards suggested , was lost on rock critics themselves. "Nostalgists all, they could be counted on once again to champion Springsteen, particularly after a long period in which there had been precious few new rock sensations to set a critic's pen flying."

One former golden boy quite familiar with the starmaking machinery had his doubts about the extent of Bruce's ability and the effect of the "hype."

"This Bruce Springsteen stuff drives me crazy," Steve Stills commented at the end of 1975. "I wouldn't want to be him for all the money in the world. He's good, but he's not all that different from a lot of other people out there. I think he's got development to go through. He's nowhere as good as his hype."

Wry and whiskey-voiced urban deadbeat Tom Waits showed his own brand of en-

thusiasm after catching one Springsteen show in Philadelphia. "Man," growled Waits, "when he was done I was layin' there in a puddle o' beer."

Warner Brothers President Joe Smith was among those who kept his hosannahs under control when *Born to Run* came out. "He's a hot new artist now," Smith said of Springsteen, "but he's not the new messiah and I question whether he will establish an international mania. He's got a very long way to go before he does what Elton has done, or Rod Stewart or The Rolling Stones or Led Zeppelin."

With his Roxy engagement behind him, Bruce had an opportunity for something he'd always wanted to do; he finally met "wall of sound" originator Phil Spector.

Spector was at Gold Star Recording Studios in Hollywood, familiar turf for him, and he was in the process of producing a single for Dion. Spector had heard *Born to Run*; his reported reaction was "I'm mildly interested, I'm hip to what the kid is doing." He was interested enough to invite Springsteen to the Dion session.

Bruce arrived with Miami Steve, who had once played

with Dion. As *Rolling Stone* reported, Bruce walked in and "Spector fixed him with his notorious size-up stare. But then Phil offered his hand and said, 'You're a very talented man'. The ice was broken."

Springsteen stayed for five hours, remaining mostly quiet while Spector ran the show. Goodnaturedly, he quipped to his musicians, "okay, fellas, Bruce Spring-street is here. He's on the cover of *Time* and he's born to run, so let's show him how to make a record."

Spector also goaded Bruce with "how could a kid like you be a Wasp with such a Jewish name?" and noted as Bruce departed "if I were with you your records would be clear and better and you'd sell five times as many."

When the historic meeting was over, someone suggested it had been a bit like Sandy Koufax being introduced to Don Sutton. Not quite, said Spector. "It's more like Babe Ruth and Hank Aaron."

Bruce's distate and disinterest in the business end of his career is well documented. "It takes a lot of the fun out of it. I've got people I pretty much trust," he said in March of '75. "If I was writin' songs to become a businessman, I'd become a businessman.

Of his oft-criticized manager, Bruce acknowledged "they probably don't like him. But, what can I say? I like the guy. I like Mike Appel because he is very responsive. They don't understand."

Naturally, plenty of people wanted a piece of this hot property· and advice was plentiful if not cheap. "I've had a million guys come up

and say, 'Hey, man, let me manage you, put you on tour with the Who, I'll put you on tour with the Rolling Stones, in front of eight billion people, and you'll be famous tomorrow, and we'll make a lot of money and be rich.' "

Bruce asserted, "That's not my scene. My scene is, 'I'll bring the band in, we play as long as we want, and we present what we have to present.' "

Springsteen tends to do what he wants, not what the rules of the trade want. One Columbia exec told *Gallery* that despite the poor production of the first two albums, Bruce was incredibly knowledgeable about the studio and "he has a great ear. The problem is that he's more interested in learning than in documenting what he's learned. He does not cater to marketing."

'When I was growing up, the only thing that never let me down was rock 'n' roll," Springsteen has stated. "Like, rock 'n' roll came to my house where there seemed to be no way out. It just seemed like a dead end street."

No one understands better than Bruce that music could be a form of deliverance. "It reached down into all those homes where there was no music or books or any kind of creative sense, and it infiltrated the whole thing. That's what happened in my house."

For many rock fans, Bruce was the medium's most accomplished messenger; they felt, during his long hiatus, that a part of their own lives had been taken away; he had become that important to some people. His own description of the effects music had in his life matches how

many young folks of the late '70s would describe *his* significance in *their* lives. "Rock 'n' roll, man, it changed my life," he's said. "It was like, you know, the 'Voice of America', the *real* America, coming into your home. It was the liberating, the out, the key out of the pits. Once I found the guitar I had the key to the highway!"

Bruce acknowledges the impact a musician can make. "The Beatles opened doors," he surmises. "Ideally, if any stuff I do could ever do that for somebody, that's the best. Can't do anything better than that. Rock 'n' roll motivates. It's the big gigantic motivator, at least it was for me."

He remembers, "I think my first experience seeing a rock star was going to Steve Paul's Scene and seeing Johnny Winter. That was really something. I remember between sets, he came out and sat at the very next table from me and my friends.

That memory is a fond one, but Bruce has often indicated that he himself is not interested in being a rock *star* per se. He has called rock stars jokes, gyps, and hoaxes. In *Melody Maker,* he once explained "they're just people who wanna crawl back in the womb, people who have built their own reality and are afraid of reality itself."

"They let all the other things become more important than playing," he believes. "Playing is the important thing. Once you forget that, you've had it."

He recalls, "when I was a kid, what mattered to me more than the performance was the power of the music. People

KEN REGAN / CAMERA 5

Bruce and Karen Darbin

emphasize the personal too much. Being a rock star, that's the booby prize. Me, I set out to be a rock 'n' roller.''

Rock is his religion, and Bruce even has his own version of Moses' tablets. In concert he tells a long story about how Moses didn't stick around to find out about an eleventh commandment. The missing edict from heaven, says Bruce, was "Let It Rock!"

If Bruce appears to be an indomitable spirit, it is obvious where his strength stems from. "Rock 'n' roll's never about giving up," he swears. "For me—for a lot of kids—it was a totally positive force not optimistic all the time, but positive. It was never—never about surrender." It is precisely that feeling, that positive energy and mental uplift so long missing, that Bruce has restored to modern popular music.

And his gift for music has also enabled Bruce to live something close to the life he chooses; it may have seemed that that control and freedom was threatened for awhile, but Springsteen never lost sight of its importance.

"I know what it's like not to be able to do want you want to do, 'cause when I go home that's what I see," Bruce explained to *Creem* interviewer Robert Duncan. "It's no fun. It's no joke. I see my sister and her husband. They're living the lives of my parents in a certain kind of way. They got kids, they're working hard. They're just real nice, real soulful people. These are people you can see something in their eyes. It's really something. I know a lot of people back there"

Bruce added, "I asked my sister, 'What do you do for fun?' 'I don't have any fun', she says. She wasn't kidding.''

For an excruciatingly long time, Bruce was prevented from doing what *he* wanted to do. Album number four was not just around the corner and ready in 1976; it

79

Bruce and Ronnie Spector, 1977

would not appear until the middle of 1978.

Almost a year of that interim would be taken up by a legal battle between Springsteen and Mike Appel. It is a matter that neither has discussed much in public; such silence is often part of the settlement. But it is known that Appel began to resent Jon Landau's growing influence on his client. The time came to sever the Springsteen-Appel arrangement, but the parting was not an easy one. One major outcome was that Appel maintained the rights to the early Springsteen songs.

Bruce's protracted legal battles were followed by an eleven-month stint in the studio as he put the finishing touches on *Darkness on the Edge of Town.* The net result was that nearly three years elapsed before any new Springsteen product reached the listening audience.

To many who were unaware of the true situation, Bruce's absence added fuel to arguments that he had not been worthy of the "hype" that greeted *Born to Run,* that he was a flash in the pan who had never caught on and had faded into much deserved obscurity. It was even being whispered that some magazines felt they had been wrongly taken in by the Springsteen hoopla and would be wary of jumping on any subsequent bandwagon.

The fact that these were misconceptions that ignored virtually any of the facts at hand did not prevent them from becoming disturbingly prevalent notions. Such stories ignored the fact that Bruce had not released a follow-up to *Born to Run* because he was prohibited from doing so, not because Columbia didn't yearn for one or because he was unwilling or artistically incapable.

In the few public appearances Bruce did make in 1977, public reception and ticket demand was as warm as ever; the concert going public still treated him as a major rock star.

People who knew Bruce only as a *Time* and *Newsweek* cover boy and didn't really follow his career from 1976 onward also seemed to forget that *Born to Run* had, to the ears of most critics and millions of fans, been every bit as brilliant a record as it was cracked up to be. And it had been a success, a sound investment of all those Columbia promotional dollars, reaching number one on the charts and platinum status. What's more, the original raves were genuine; they had not been "hyped."

Philadelphia disc jockey and writer Ed Sciaky, an early and ardent Springsteen booster, understood the adverse reaction of the less-informed. "If you haven't seen him, you really don't think that it's all probable that there's anyone that's this good, let alone him," he explained. "He's so good that if you tell it like it is, it sounds like it can't be true. The business is known for hypes and if someone is being touted as being this good, you know no one can be that good so, therefore, he must not be very good; so that people who'd never seen him resented the whole thing."

That resentment, which often took the form of laughing, deprecating comments about Springsteen, was enough to make many of his normally levelheaded partisans seethe with venom. In an interview with *Oui*, Meat Loaf's songwriter Jim Steinman, in a discussion of his musical influences and idols, became visibly upset as he spoke of the Springsteen detractors who "didn't understand" the true situation.

Between *Born to Run* and *Darkness on the Edge of Town*, about the only new

Springsteen music to see the light of day was an extremely good-natured version of "Santa Claus Is Coming to Town," which was not released commercially but found its way onto several FM radio stations.

Recorded in concert, "Santa" begins with Bruce asking Clemons if he's behaved himself, and speculating that Santa might bring him a brand new saxophone. The song is given a pretty faithful interpretation, except that Bruce is a far more gutsy and emotional singer than most Christmas carolers, and it does find room for a solo for Clarence in the middle. It concludes with a few bars of "Jingle Bells" for good measure. It made a delightful addition to FM holiday play lists, and should become a rock classic of the yuletide season.

In the absence of Bruce himself, his music did come to us in varied and roundabout ways. From the Asbury Park scene Springsteen had exposed to the universe came another act, Southside Johnny and the Asbury Jukes, a bar band much in the mold of Boston's J. Geils Band. Johnny Lydon, he of the wonderfully wizened voice, was a longtime chum of Bruce's, and one of the band's first big numbers was a Springsteen composition, "You Mean So Much to Me Baby."

That song also featured vocals by Ronnie Spector, in what amounted to a comeback by the ex-leader of the Ronettes ("Be My Baby") and former wife of production wizard Phil Spector. As she told *Crawdaddy* writer Richard Price, Jimmy Iovine, the engineer for John Lennon

and Springsteen, "called me one night and he asked me to come down to a session (for Southside Johnny's first album). I wasn't doing anything that evening, and it was right up the street, so why not, you know? So I went down there, and I liked 'You Mean So Much'. So Bruce Springsteen came in that night. He had written it for a guy but he rewrote it for a girl."

Bruce was a longtime worshipper of Ronnie; an autographed poster of her is said to be one of his most treasured possessions. Giving her his song effectively ended her retirement. She went on tour with the Jukes, singing several songs in concert. And her first single, "Say Goodbye to Hollywood," was produced by Steve Van Zandt (who wrote the flip side, "Baby Please Don't Go) and backed up by the entire E Street Band. On the sleeve of the single, Ronnie embraces Bruce, sheepishly grinning beneath his shades.

The sounds of the *Born to Run* album are still so fresh, and perhaps so definitively produced, arranged, and executed, that no cover versions of any of the eight tunes emerged. However, renditions of songs on *Greetings from Asbury Park, N.J.* and *The Wild, the Innocent, and the E Street Shuffle* began to proliferate.

Many of the early Springsteen songs would probably defy interpretation by another artist, and we have yet to see any Las Vegas crooner attempt them on the "Tonight Show." However, two of the more approachable tunes would have to be "For You" on the first album and "4th of July, As-

81

bury Park (Sandy)" on the second.

"For You" was covered by The Greg Kihn Band, a Berkeley outfit recording for the aptly titled Beserkley label. Kihn's version was passable if not startling. Bruce wrote and sang "I came for you, for you, I came for you, but you did not need my urgency," and apparently neither did Kihn. Bruce's vocal is stamped "urgent"; Kihn's more joyously celebrates the fact that he has come. In concert, Bruce has dedicated "For You" to Kihn.

"Sandy," as the song with the unwieldy title has come to be called, received a treatment from the Hollies, a commercially viable group with a string of hit singles stretching back more than a decade. Noted for their harmonies, the Hollies hit all the right notes on this one, but compared to Bruce's sensitive rendering theirs is pretty tepid stuff. Antiseptic, and not one of their finer efforts.

Nevertheless, Kihn and the Hollies are to be thanked for keeping Bruce's work before at least a portion of the public during his absence. But the man who did the most to champion the cause of Springsteendom was Manfred Mann, whose group carried his own name since their first English hit in 1964.

Mann's varied repertoire over the years included reworked Dylan material, most notably the highly successful single "The Mighty Quinn." He began to do with Bruce as he had done with Bob. Mann first included Springsteen's "Spirit in the Night" on the "Nightingales and Bombers" album and followed with a

recording of "Blinded by the Light" which proved to be one of the best selling singles.

"Blinded," of course, was perhaps the most lyrically complex song Bruce Springsteen ever wrote. As initially recorded, the scattershot barrage of images would have been tough for Top 40 to accommodate.

Mann completely rearranged the music, making it replete with "hooks."

The single was shaped in such a way as to give greater emphasis, and maybe a stronger focus, to some of the lyrics, wheras Bruce's singing had breezed by in a dazzling but hard to handle stream. Certain lyrics sounded a bit awkward when Mann chose to repeat them at dramatic interludes, but his method was essentially effective. His "Blinded by the Light" was certainly one of the better and less bland singles of the period, a wringer and attention grabber. Subtle he was not; his "Spirit" was far more nocturnally malevolent than Bruce's, and his being "Blinded by the Light" seemed much more cause for alarm.

Manfred Mann explained his approach to Springsteen's material in a conversation with Philadelphia writer Don Waller, citing his knack for "finding good songs and doing them in a way that is very different from the original, and throwing a completely different light on the song, seeing it in a completely different angle. Like putting it up to a distorted mirror; it becomes something completely different."

So it was—so totally unlike Bruce's original music as to seem that *Greetings from As-*

bury Park, N.J. had been totally reprogrammed through a computer. There were some who considered the results too abominable, but they were not a majority. "You would almost expect the reaction to be negative, because it you like somebody and you're familiar with how they've done a song, it's kind of strange to hear someone else do it completely different," Mann noted. It must be remembered, however, that *Greetings* was not a chart topper for Springsteen, and that many people were hearing "Blinded by the Light" for the first time. They lacked any basis for comparison.

Manfred believed Bruce was himself pleased. "Dylan used to like the way we did his stuff. And I think it's because I have no respect for the original—I just treat it with a total lack of respect. I'm making the record, I don't give a damn what the guy meant, what he was trying to do. I mean he did it, it's not up to me to do it the way he did it."

Apparently Mann wanted Bruce to sing on the revamped "Blinded" and he heard Bruce was interested, but Mann was in England and Bruce was in the southern United States and they never connected. "It's a drag," notes Mann, "because at the end of the song when the verse and chorus run simultaneously, I wanted him to sing the verse. That would have been nice. But, in the end I sang it."

What would have been a compelling duo never materialized, but the product was important to Springsteen's career nevertheless. The single "Born to Run" had made

82

it to the low 20s on national Top 40 charts, but Manfred Mann's single made it big in far more markets. It was for many listeners the first exposure ever to Springsteen music. It was a reminder that Bruce was still around, that his music was palatable, and that there was a big and potentially bigger audience for it. If Manfred Mann did nothing more than to keep the word of Bruce alive, he deserves thanks.

In the days *Darkness on the Edge of Town* was being recorded, Bruce became close friends with photographer Lynn Goldsmith, and started fiddling with a camera himself.

"He came in and looked at a picture on my wall and said he was a big Ansel Adams fan, and Ansel's name wasn't even on the picture," Goldsmith told *American Photographer* magazine. She began to instruct Bruce in the use of the camera. "He learned very fast. He's such a sensitive guy."

Bruce took pictures of his E Street pals and of Lynn Goldsmith; *American Photographer* printed a lovely color portrait Springsteen shot of her. His shots of the band may appear in a photo book, of which he is the main subject, at a future date.

Someone as conscientious about his records and as anxi-

ous to bring his music to his fans in live concert as Bruce is doesn't have much time to pursue other interests, but softball is apparently one. "We used to play hard," he recalls. "We had to stop, though, when Clarence and myself used to get too battered up. We'd go on stage all wracked up and it would *hurt.*"

And as would only be natural for a man who spent so much time on the Asbury Park boardwalk with its amusement centers and penny arcades (which always cost more than a penny), Bruce is partial to pinball. John Scher conveniently installed a machine backstage at the

Captiol during Bruce's summer 1978 tour.

Miami Steve Van Zandt, once ogling the Elton John-Pinball Wizard table, demanded to know why there wasn't a Bruce Springsteen-Born to Run machine as well. Bruce answered him. "Ya see, these guys wanna make *bucks.* You gotta be *famous.*" It should be noted that this exchange occurred just a short time before the *Time* and *Newsweek* covers surfaced.

"Playing pinball is just like giggling," observes Springsteen. "Some nights you go out there and it's dynamite, and other times you just don't score. One summer I

had just two dollars a day spending money. I'd save one dollar for pinball." At five cents a game in Asbury, that could last you until the sun set over the boardwalk.

And of course, as anyone who's heard even one Springsteen tune could tell, cars are a passion. "I love drivin' around in my car when I'm 26 and I'll love drivin' around in my car when I'm 36," he said in 1975. "Those aren't irrelevant feelings for me."

Thus far, at least, marriage has not been one of Bruce's pasttimes, In '75 he told Dave Marsh, "I lived with someone once for two years. But I decided that to be married, you had to write married

music. And I'm not ready for that." Carly and James and Kris and Rita, take note.

In time, Bruce found that being his own lead guitarist restricted him somewhat in performance. He was interested in developing his role as lead singer; that was the chief reason why he brought old buddy Miami Steve Van Zandt aboard.

When the change occurred, Bruce minimized its significance. "No, no, it was no big deal," he told *Hit Parader.* "Putting a guitar down is no big deal. One difference is you ain't holding it in your hand and you ain't making noise.

"It's no big incredible

84

changeover or nothing," he reassured interviewer Joseph Rose. "I felt like that's what I had to do next, so I'm gonna do it. It keeps it interesting for me. I always like to keep it like alive, never let the band go to sleep on stage, always throwing them some curve balls so they got to be awake all the time."

Bruce said of the new addition; "I'd known Steve for years and years, since we were 16. We played together in countless other bands. At the time I started this band, I just couldn't afford a guitar player. I tried to keep it down to as small a membership as I could. And, like, I'd never hire a guy because he was my friend, you know, unless it's a guy like Steve, who is a very talented guy in his own way." Bruce was merely keeping it in the family. "He's a local, man. If you keep with the cats around your town and the people that you grew up with, then you maintain your essence."

Comradery and friendship are an important part of musicianship to Springsteen. "When there's a guy you've known a lot of years there and he knows what you've been through and you know what he's been through, and you've both been through a lot of those same things together, you've sat in them bars wondering where it was gonna go down and then he's there and it's coming down then, you know, there's nothing that can replace that kind of stuff," Bruce surmises.

Leaving most of the guitar-work to Steve was not a decision that tore Bruce apart. "When I play the guitar, it

ain't like there's a lot of solos and stuff going on all the time. It's like, the only guy that really solos in Clarence," he explained. "Most of the time we're playing as a band playing songs with relatively few solos."

The final impetus to become a front man like "all the great singers" came from a trip Bruce and Steve took to "some dumpy bar down in South Jersey" to see the old soul team of Sam and Dave. To Bruce, "they're so hooked up together and just two of the most graceful cats you've ever seen on stage."

"It's just great to front," Bruce believes. "Like in the early '60s there were some great front men. Like Paul Jones with Manfred Mann. I always loved that guy, thought he was fantastic. Man, when they came out and did 'Do Wah Diddy Diddy'— we do some of their songs, you know ("Sha La La" and "Pretty Flamingo" on occasion in concert—I loved them. I love all their songs. I thought he was a great, great singer, Paul Jones. He has this great distinctive voice that I'm nuts about."

The example of men like Jones, Jagger, Sam and Dave, Eric Burdon, and Jackie Wilson prodded Bruce to go up front. "Plus it's a little easier to lead the band without the guitar. You can get a little better picture of what you're going for."

It's what he wants to do, but Bruce stresses about performing, "it's never easy. It may look easy, but it ain't; it's never easy."

He observes, "It can be a lot of fun, which it is most of the time, because if it wasn't

I would probably do something else. I guess. And it can be . . . it can be lots of things. Sometimes it's fun. Sometimes it ain't fun but it's still good. But it's just never easy, really. And I don't think it should be."

It is because he would never short change his followers that Springsteen makes that kind of statement. But more often than not, he gets as much back as the enormous amount he gives out. "It's the stage thing, that rush moment that you live for."

"We were all playing anything we could to be part of the scene." Van Zandt remembers of the time he met Springsteen. "Bruce was writing five or ten songs a week. He would say, 'I'm gonna go home tonight and write a great song,' and he did. He was the Boss then, and he's the Boss now."

In concert, The Boss frequently fills in the gaps, and gives the E Street Band members a rest, with rambling, off the cuff tales of New Jersey street life, or of the background for a song he is about to sing. There are plenty of pauses, repeats, and digressions, but the narration is always fascinating. He is creating up there, and he is sharing a little extra with the audience. Bruce is a gifted storyteller; his monologues are often as visually rich as his songs.

A typical example is this one, from the stage of the Capitol Theatre in Passaic, New Jersey last year. From the gritty confines of the Garden State, fans are suddenly on the road and searching with Bruce:

"There was this Robert Mitchum movie—it was about these moonshine runners down south. I never saw the movie, I only saw the poster in the lobby of the theatre. I took the title and I wrote this song. I didn't think there was ever a place that was like what I wrote in this song. I didn't know if there was or not.

"And we were out in the desert over the summertime driving through Nevada. And we came upon this house on the side of the road. It had a picture of Geronimo, with the land-lord, it said 'landlord' over the top. It had a big sign (that said) 'this is the land of peace, love, justice, and no mercy' and it pointed down this little dirt road that said 'Thunder Road.'"

Bruce can be remarkably insouciant and candid with his audiences. Once he paused between songs and enthralled a throng of 600 with a detailed treatise on how he and his E Street pals used to run afoul of the Mafiosos when they played in New Jersey. Then, as an afterthought, Bruce added "now hey, that's in confidence. I wouldn't want that to go outside this room."

Bruce didn't actually put New Jersey on the map—it had never been quite as obscure as, say, Delaware. Yet he did remove some tarnish from its soiled reputation as a string of smoke-belching refineries and decaying small cities. As one writer observed, it was now fashionable to be from the "armpit" of the nation.

Bruce also did more than any single figure to revive rock and roll as a New Jersey industry. There had always

Bruce didn't put New Jersey on the map but he did remove some tarnish from its soiled reputation.

been bars he and his mates scuffled in, a scene which also provided a refuge for plenty of big name '60s acts on the way down. There was also a reasonably healthy black music scene, of which the enduring native-born Isley Brothers were the most prominent figures.

None of those venues, however, did much to attract the semi-affluent, white, largely suburban audience from which concert promoters make their bread and butter. Bruce had that kind of pull, and almost simultaneously with his rise a string of medium-sized concert halls, offering headline rock acts, began to spring up in the Garden State.

The showplace of rock in New Jersey became John Scher's Capitol Theatre in Passaic. Local boy Scher, who is still only twenty-eight, was coming into his own before Bruce had been heard from; he'd staged outdoor concerts in Jersey City as early as 1972, and he'd opened the Capitol with acts like Humble Pie and Mountain.

There's no doubt, however,

that Springsteen is the Capitol's most popular performer and that his appearances there have done much to enhance the hall's reputation. In the midst of his legal doldrums, Bruce made a memorable and much talked about guest appearance at a Southside Johnny show on New Year's Eve, 1977. His summer 1978 show at the Capitol was treated as a major event by New York progressive station WNEW-FM, which broadcast the show as part of a small network that stretched as far as Maryland.

Scher acknowledges Bruce's power to convert the multitudes. "I like to take somebody who's never seen rock and roll and bring 'em into my theatre for a Springsteen show," he has said. "In twenty minutes, they're on their feet clapping. Twenty minutes later they're screaming, twenty minutes after that they're on their chairs, and twenty minutes later they're fucking freaking out."

Bruce's 1978 birthday was spent on stage at the Capitol where, to his surprise, a scantily attired young woman popped out of a huge cake.

His return to Passaic in 1978 was full of poignancy. For Bruce it was a simple matter; "long time no see," he greeted the crowd.

One mainstay of Springsteen performances may throw the fear of God into some of his concerned fans. It is known as the "stretcher" routine.

In this episode, our energetic hero sings his heart out, exhausts himself totally, and has to be removed from the premises by stretcher bearers. But never-say-die Bruce breaks away, pops up again, and returns to his microphone. Finally, he is taken away by force.

"We got it from James Brown," Bruce told *The Aquarian* interviewer. "He used to get himself so worked up that the bassist led him off stage wrapped in a cape. He'd throw the cape off his shoulders and come running back to the mike stand some two or three times. It drove 'em wild. So that's where we got the idea for the stretcher routine."

Springsteen has only featured his own compositions on his four albums, but his stage shows are peppered with songs by other artists that were on the airways when Bruce was an adolescent. They're mainly soul tunes and British rockers from the early '60s, but Bruce steadfastly refuses to refer to them as "oldies."

"Whenever a song's got that life, that ability to move you and that is still very relevant to today, to what's happening, that's important," Bruce explained in a Chicago interview. "We don't play no oldies. They may be older songs, but

JAMES SHIVE

they're not nostalgic, really. I was never into that whole nostalgic thing—because it's stupid. But these songs are different, and it's obvious by the reaction they get. It's great today, it's great right now, and if somebody plays it and people hear it, they'll still love it."

Others would agree that Bruce is not merely recycling old material. *Stereo Review*, which, incidentally, gave *Greetings from Asbury Park N.J.* its Best of The Year award in 1973, later observed "probably the greatest compliment I can pay him is to say that when he sandwiches 'Route 66' and 'Then She Kissed Me' in between his own numbers, they sound like *his* songs, as if *he* wrote them."

There has been talk of a live Bruce Springsteen album for years now. Springsteen fanatics who couldn't sway their friends on the basis of the Boss' recorded work would always dangle the carrot: "Wait until you see him in concert."

Some observers felt "Born to Run" captured some of Springsteen's stage dynamism, but almost every Springsteen adherent wants a concert set to vinyl.

Mike Appel was talking about it way back in 1975. "We want it to be a two-and-half to three-hour album, just like a concert," he suggested.

It didn't come out of the long tour that followed the completion of "Born to Run," but Springsteen was taping several of his 1978 shows and spending spare time reviewing the tapes, so the project is obviously still getting serious consideration.

Bruce was long in giving us

89

RICHARD McCAFFREE

a follow-up to *Born to Run*, but his presence was heavily felt in the interim period from 1976 to 1978. In fact, in terms of its impact on the sound of contemporary music, its role in shaping the directions both established and rising artists would take, *Born to Run* ranks as the most influential popular album since David Bowie's *The Rise and Fall of Ziggy Stardust and the Spiders from Mars,* the trail blazing 1972 set.

Springsteen, more than any single individual, once again cessful album. (In fact, Seger and Springsteen are avid mutual admirers, and friends have suggested that the reason Detroit was one of Bruce's last conquests and the New York-Philadelphia area one of Seger's last ones was because each place was considered to be the other man's homeground, and they respectfully deigned not to tread on each other's turf.

Running through the streets of the city, being streetwise, hanging out on the corner, and the whole urban adoles- as a purveyor of casual ballads and telling sagas of plights of being young and stuck in suburbia. His greatest success, however, came when he shifted his focus to New York City. By the time he released *52nd Street,* Joel's Columbia biography stressed "Billy Joel is closer to the streets than ever." (Springsteen, by the way, like Dylan, has never had an official Columbia biography). By November of 1978, *52nd Street* was the top selling album in America. Jim Miller of *New Times* suggested Joel

> *Springsteen fanatics who couldn't sway their friends on the basis of the Boss' recorded work would always dangle the carrot: "Wait until you see him in concert."*

established rock as an urban sound. The lore of modern music again became the adventures and pitfalls of city life.

Other artists began to embrace some of the elements that had made Springsteen the latest rave. Bob Seger, a perennial regional favorite in the midwest, finally made it to national superstardom (deservedly so) with *Night Moves,* the title song of which was the outstanding single of 1977. One rock writer suggested Seger had listened to Springsteen and learned how to make a suc- cent mode of behavior became fashionable again for adults, especially rock fans in their twenties and thirties. It became advisable to incorporate part of the city image into one's own album. Genya Ravan, a former star with the jazz rock outfit Ten Wheel Drive and later a producer of punk recording acts, favored a raw rock sound on her return to recording after a long hiatus. She called her effort *Urban Desire,* which is just what Bruce instilled in the hearts of men and women.

Billy Joel, who is in fact from Long Island, started out was "working the same vein of class-conscious urban romanticism mined by Bruce Springsteen."

One of the more interesting success stories of 1978 was Meat Loaf, whose record "Bat Out Of Hell" gained popularity slowly and steadily until reaching its peak and platinum status almost a year after its release.

Its release came at a time when Springsteen had not released a new album for over a year and wasn't going to do so in the foreseeable future. Meat Loaf and the writer of all his songs, Jim Steinman, dedi-

Bruce and Bob Seger at Pine Knob in Detroit, 1978

cated the title song to Bruce Springsteen, and E Streeters Roy Bittan and Max Weinberg played on the album. Meat Loaf's album is full of teen dreams; it was Springsteen who had made adolescent yearning fashionable once again.

As the public awaited Bruce's fourth disc, it was granted the first by Billy Falcon, *Burning Rose*. By his phrasing, his vocal gimmickry, and his instrumentation, Falcon so obviously imitated Springsteen as to almost be a parody. It was striking how the copy paled in comparison with the original; Falcon

only succeeded in making the absence of Springsteen more painful.

While Bruce was at work in the studio on *Darkness on the Edge of Town*, Mike Appel had also recovered from their litigation and had a new wunderkind, Arlyn Gale, whose ABC release *Back to the Midwest Night* was ready at about the same time as *Darkness*.

Gale is actually quite good; he knows how to construct a song, he understands that music is supposed to be exciting, and part of the time, at least, he gives us something original.

There are times, however, when he seems like a Springsteen clone; since he's Springsteen's stand-in, that's hardly shocking. The title track in particular dredges up all the old Springsteen saws about driving around, pursuing girls, looking for something to do and heading off into the night. The only differences are that Bruce's night is in New Jersey or New York while Arlyn's is midwestern; Bruce would invoke the name of Roy Orbison to establish time and place, while Arlyn favors Gene Pitney.

The final irony is Arlyn Gale's album cover. In a haze,

91

With Patti Smith

with his arms folded, standing in the dusk with his head bent down a bit into his chest, the guy looks like no one but a young Springsteen.

Arlyn Gale is actually a twenty-five-year-old from a farm community. Woodstock, Illinois is sixty miles from Chicago and twenty miles from the Wisconsin border. Arlyn attended a Catholic high school, where he was voted "Mr. Cool" by his classmates.

Gale, whose first public performance was at a 4-H talent show, played small venues across the country and was seeking a recording contract when he earned an appointment with Mike Appel. He played live in Appel's office; most recording execs would have asked for a demo and stuck it at the bottom of a pile.

It is almost inevitable that Gale would be compared to Springsteen, but he calls himself "a cross between Mimmie Rodgers and Carlo Buti" (the "yodelin' cowboy" and the Italian crooner). According to Gale, Appel was so anxious to avoid comparisons between Gale and Springsteen that on one song in which a sax solo seemed proper he overruled it, because he felt it would remind people of Clarence Clemons.

"Once I'm on the road a little and show that we're different personalities, it'll pass," Gale says of the Springsteen analogies.

With the finishing touches going onto the fourth album, Bruce tested the waters a bit by sharing his musicianship with a couple of promising artists who could certainly use the material.

Poetess Patti Smith, a friend to many a rock star and a real life heroine to some people in the New York metro area, was the beneficiary of one of the most diehard cult followings known to rock. Alas, this did not translate into big album sales. By 1978 Patti, an energetic, sometimes volatile personality, needed more than a few well wishers; she needed a hit record. She got together with Bruce in a collaboration made perhaps not in heaven, but headed for "the charts." They coauthored "Because the Night"—roughly, it broke down to Bruce's music and Patti's words—and Patti's recording of it was a nationwide Top Ten single. The success saved her career, for the time being.

Rockabilly crooner Robert Gordon, teaming with pioneer rock guitarist Link Wray, had some, but not enormous, success with his material evocative of Presley, Holly, and the best of early rock. But the number of poeple who knew of Robert Gordon was probably quadrupled after he recorded Bruce's "Fire," a pensive, dramatic tune about midnight rambling. It wasn't as big a success as "Because the Night," but it was certainly the high point of Gordon's career.

The prognosis for *Darkness on the Edge of Town* had to be considered excellent. Bruce appeared to have the Midas touch. Two of his new tunes had turned, if not to gold, to something quite precious and valuable. There was a hankering for Bruce out there.

Rarely had there been more riding on the imminent re-

lease of a record album than there was in the case of Bruce's fourth, *Darkness on the Edge of Town.* It had been so long since *Born to Run,* and his mental energies had largely been diverted to matters that were not musical. His partisans had to wonder if he would deliver the promise of brilliance that *Born to Run* seemed to carry. His doubters had to be convinced that he wasn't just a flash in the pan, that Bruce Springsteen wasn't already yesterday's hero.

If the 1975 media blitz hadn't mushroomed so severely around Springsteen, perhaps *Darkness on the Edge of Town* could have been treated as just another album release. But now Bruce Springsteen lived in a goldfish bowl; every step he made would be closely scrutinized.

No one had been more overwhelmed by the media blitz than Bruce himself, as he reflected when *Darkness on the Edge of Town* finally did come out. "When all the attention started, I was out in L.A. and Jack Nicholson came to a show," Bruce noted in a *Time* interview. "I asked him how he handled the attention. He said, for him, it was a long time coming and he was mostly glad to have it. I didn't quite see it that way. I bundled it all together into one general experience and labeled it 'bad'. I felt control over my life and career was slipping away and that all the attention was, like, an obstacle. But that was a mistake. After a while, I realized, well, time was on my side. Whatever happens, I wasn't gonna go away. I got no place to go."

In fact, it enhanced the

With Robert Gordon

image of the man that he, almost alone, realized that time was on his side. As they had with baseball's Ted Williams, who missed several seasons during two wars, and Muhammed Ali, whose career was interrupted for three years by ramifications of his refusal to be drafted, people were suggesting that Bruce was being sidetracked during his peak period, that he was being prevented from creating during what should have been his most fruitful years.

While writers and fans frothed at the bit about the tragedy of talent going to waste, Bruce alone seemed to understand that there were plenty of "fruitful days" ahead. He seemed a paragon of patience, less desperate and anxious about rushing ahead than most in his growing circle of well wishers.

Many were stupified when the legal hassles with Mike Appel were finally resolved in the summer of '77 and Bruce didn't immediately rush out an album in two or three months. The Boss knew he had time; he understood that he "wasn't gonna go away."

"I knew it was just a matter of time," he tells the *Aquarian.* "We were playing almost throughout that whole episode even though we weren't supposed to. I mean, what kind of law is it that is written specifically to stop a man from doing what he does to make his money?"

Bruce added, "The only really frustrating thing which did cause me grief was the fact that my songs weren't my own. I didn't own my songs. That hurt.

"You know when you go into one of these things that you're gonna fight someone for a year," Springsteen matter-of-factly told Peter Knobler after his legal battles with Appel was completed. "Every day, toe-to-toe, face-to-face combat. You're gonna wanna kill him and he's gonna wanna kill you. That's what it's all about, depositions. And it takes its toll. But on the other hand, it's still a guy that you . . . kinda . . . like—and you know he . . . kinda . . . likes you."

The battle, to Bruce, was a matter in which principle was more important than money. Of his one time manager he said "he worked hard for a long time—we all worked hard—and he sacrificed and, OK, he deserved something for it. But what I wanted was the thing itself: my songs. It got so where, if I wrote a book, I couldn't even quote my own lyrics—I couldn't quote 'Born to Run'! That whole period of my life just seemed to be out of my hands. That's why I started playing music in the

first place—to control my life. No way was I gonna let that get away."

Springsteen never had any interest in the business end of his music career; even in his minor bands in the old days, he'd leave that to Miami Steve or someone else. So he didn't see the future implications of his original contract with Appel, in which all publishing rights were granted to Mike.

"I didn't know what publishing *was,*" Bruce would comment afterward. "You're gonna think it's what happens to books. It's one of those words. I knew no one who had ever made a record before. I knew absolutely no one who had ever had any contact whatsoever with the music business."

Springsteen is a unique individual, and there are certain aspects of his personality that perhaps served as a buffer against doldrums that could justifiably have set in during 1976 and 1977.

"I'm not a planning-type guy," notes Bruce. "You can't count on nothing in this life. I never have expectations when I get involved in things. That way, I never have disappointments."

The financial loss he suffered during the litigation with Appel was apparently more important to other folks than it was to Springsteen. "It has nothing to do with money," Springsteen said in *Crawdaddy.* "Money is the form it takes but it had nothing to do with money. Not to me, anyway. I'm more alive than I ever was, and *that* is the story."

That was part of what he was trying to say on *Darkness of the Edge of Town.* The

interim period was not a complete waste for Springsteen; there was growth of a kind going on. "I had a big awakening in the past two, three years," he noted. "Much bigger than people would think. Learned a lot of things, saw a lot of things. Realized a lot of things about my own past. So it's there on the record."

The fact that the recording sessions for *Darkness* took almost a full year was no cause for alarm as far as the Boss himself was concerned. "You owe your best," Bruce maintains. "I just couldn't understand why people would rush to get out an album by a particular date and then regret it afterward.

"You see what matters to the kids," he explains. "They want to have the stuff, but if it's not the best you can do, it's not worth doing. Not for me anyway."

During sessions for *Darkness,* Bruce often stayed at the Hotel Navarro in Manhattan and went virtually unrecognized. He was sans beard, and the public still was thinking of him as the bearded *Born to Run* tough.

The engineer for *Darkness,* as with *Born to Run,* was Jimmie Iovine, who is still only twenty-five but already a respected electronics expert. Iovine believes that along with John Lennon, Elvis, and Rod Stewart, Springsteen has one of the four greatest rock 'n' roll voices ever.

The original working title of the fourth album was *Badlands,* but there was already an album ready for release under that title by Bill Chinnock. Chinnock just happens to be an Asbury Park native and a

95

buddy of Bruce's. The Boss reportedly asked Bill if he thought his releasing a record with the same title would cause the newcomer some problems, and Chinnock responded that frankly, it would. Magnanimously, Bruce opted for a new title.

A long search for the perfect photographic locale had been conducted in conjunction with the *Badlands* title. However, when that was scrapped, Bruce opted for very simple shots of himself on the cover of *Darkness on the Edge of Town.* He looks as if he has just gotten up, and that is reportedly the case. The pictures were taken by Frank Stefanko, "a friend of mine from south Jersey who works full-time in a meat market. The shots were taken at his house. He's a great photographer."

Columbia's ad campaign for *Darkness* was far more modest than the *Born to Run* push. There were no wild slogans; perhaps there no longer had to be. But it was acknowledged that Springsteen was sensitive to charges of overselling himself. All they did this time was let people know the album was out, and that's all they had to do. People had waited long enough; they wanted it and it went platinum immediately.

Just as a giant twenty-five-foot blowup of him and Clarence had towered over part of Los Angeles to promote *Born to Run,* a similar billboard promoted *Darkness on the Edge of Town.* It featured a poorly framed, poorly reproduced copy of the Stefanko shot; Bruce considered it repulsively ugly.

The *Darkness* billboard hung above a seven-story building. In a hastily prepared raid, Springsteen, Clemons, Tallent, tour manager Jim McHale, and a few other crew members rushed to the scene, gained easy access to the roof. Bruce, Garry, and Clarence, with black spray paint, emblazoned "Prove It All Night" across the billboard, and Bruce, on Clarence's mighty shoulders, added "E Street" above "Night." Plans to give the Bruce portrait a huge mustache aborted when someone thought the cops were coming.

By the middle of '78, Bruce had thirty tunes available for an album. Bruce's priorities for selection for *Darkness* were, in his words, "those I felt were the most important for me to get out. I wanted to put out stuff that I felt had the most substance and yet was still an album."

Bruce composed one song, "Factory," in ninety minutes. "Most of the songs were written real fast. It was just figuring out what to do with them," To give a little different feel to the album, there was a greater emphasis on guitar and a little less saxophone. "With the saxophone, there's no distance, it's right up to your face," Bruce believes. "But the guitar has always been a little cooler instrument."

Darkness was first played on Century Broadcasting stations in Los Angeles, San Francisco, St. Louis, and Detroit on May 18. The '78 tour began May 23 in Buffalo, and the album was released June 2.

To observe the contrast between the Bruce on *Born to Run* and the latter-day Bruce

of *Darkness,* one needn't look beyond the two covers.

The photograph by Eric Meola on *Born to Run* perhaps did more to cement the image of Springsteen in the minds of the American public than any music he wrote or performed. Leaning on the Big Man for physical and musical support, Bruce gave rock fans a hero and sidekick to outdo Batman and Robin or the Lone Ranger and Tonto.

Here's Bruce, bearded and leather-jacketed and standing proud and cocky with his guitar strung across his neck; it's the only banner he need fly, the only weapon he has to wield. He is everything he wants to be and a lot of what we want to be. His entire pose seems to speak what Warren Beatty said in *Bonnie and Clyde*: "Ain't life grand?"

To judge a record by its cover, life around the time of *Darkness on the Edge of Town* is far from grand. Here's Bruce in grubby tee shirt, without beard, looking neither heroic nor happy, looking a lot like you or me. He also looks a lot like he just got up, which in fact he did. The Bruce captured on Frank Stefanko's cover is not having a swell time, and as we listen to *Darkness* we perceive that the cover is an accurate reflection of what's inside.

"Badlands" is the first track on the latest Springsteen album, and it is also a frequent concert opener. It's a straight ahead basic rocker that gets right down to business; Bittan's piano opening is a gallop that carries us right into the action and is also appropriate to the western notion that the term Badlands conveys.

DAVID GAHR

This is a song that can hook you on your car radio, and Columbia picked it as the second single from the *Darkness* album.

There's "trouble in the heartland" on this tune which makes no bones about the author's weariness "for the same old played out scenes." It's thematically related to "Jungleland," but the difference here is that Bruce himself, not the Magic Rat or anybody else, is at the center of this saga.

"Badlands" sets the tone for the rest of *Darkness on the Edge of Town*. Bruce has more than a few bones to pick. In the past, he was not prone to complain about his own miseries in song; the only instance that comes to mind is "Growin' Up" with its adolescent pains, but he treated them pretty mater-of-factly.

The Bruce of "Badlands" is in more of a quandry, however. He's got "a head on collision smashin' in my guts" and he's "caught in a cross fire that I don't understand." He understands plenty, however. He's tired of waiting and settling for half of life's ante. "I want the heart, I want the soul, I want control right now."

There is a new directness to Bruce's lyrics here. He's disgusted with those who "spend your life waiting for a moment that just don't come." He knows that if you want something big it doesn't come cheap: "let the broken hearts stand as the price you've gotta pay." He's finally decided that "it ain't no sin to be glad you're alive." And, for the first time yet on

HOWARD ROSENBERG

record, he's even vindictive: I wanna find one face that ain't looking through me, I wanna find one place, I wanna spit in the face of these badlands."

The three-year hiatus didn't diminish Bruce's lyrical abilities one iota; his message could not be more clearly or emphatically stated. By the time "Badlands" is over, we know that we're in for a different ride with Springsteen this time. He's come to reaffirm the promise he displayed in 1975, but he's also come to exorcise the demons that have plagued him since then and even before that time. He's getting it all out, and hopefully he's leaving it all behind him. Cutting out losses and moving on is one of the things "Badlands" is about.

Bruce's guitar play is decidedly devilish at the beginning of "Adam Raised a Cain," one of the songs in which he attempts to make peace with his past, and with his father. He and his dad have "the same hot blood burning in our veins," they've got a little bit of the same thing eating away at them inside.

As the song progresses, Springsteen's emotional involvement with it increases. Soon it's almost like the words are strangling, but he pushes on to get 'em out:

You're born into this life paying,
for the sins of somebody else's past,
Daddy worked his whole life, for nothing but the pain,
Now he walks these empty rooms, looking for something to blame,

You inherit the sins, you inherit the flames,
Adam raised a Cain.

His father's failures and anxieties became his own, but "Daddy worked his whole life, for nothing but the pain" is a line that criticizes and warns against such a waste at the same time it indicates sorrow and sympathy for it. This is not an entirely angry undertaking; it's double-edged with remorse.

"Adam Raised a Cain" is far more disturbing than anything on *Born to Run,* and this is intensely personal stuff for Springsteen. The music is secondary to the lyrics here; in fact, "Adam Raised a Cain" reads better than it sounds, which is unusual for a Springsteen song. We'd consider this an important track because it's valuable information about someone we consider important. The question of whether it's entertaining or a good "song" is irrelevant. But if that question must be answered, the answer is "not particularly."

"Something in the Night" is the kind of song that separates Bruce's fans from his detractors. The naysayers claim he's mush-mouthed and garbled and that you can't distinguish the instruments. But his adherents know that this is real and heartfelt stuff; if "whoaoahs" work better than words and if a bit of the vocabulary is slurred, the essence and the meaning is very much intact.

"Something in the Night" has a broad setting—driving around, searching, and ultimately losing. There are lines in here, however, that will always be cited as Bruce's com-

mentary on his legal wrangles:
And there is a telling verse, sung in trembling doubletrack by Bruce, which seems to concisely summarize what Springsteen was bedeviled with as he was trying to get *Darkness* out:

You're born with nothing, and better off that way,
Soon as you've got something they send
someone to try to take it away.
Nothing is forgotten or forgiven,
when it's your last time around
I got stuff running 'round my head
That I just can't live down.

Perhaps, but putting it down on this album will help.

It's about time for some good news, time to hear of something Bruce is unequivocally positive about. It comes next in "Candy's Room," the fourth album's most compact track, and affirmative barn burner that would have fit on *Born to Run* right alongside of "Night."

The E Streeters creep into Candy's house, stealthily in the dark. The footsteps come from the rapid, muted, and remarkably even drumming of Max Weinberg, whose superiority to Springsteen's previous percussionists becomes clear here, and the tinkering of Roy Bittan, who shows again that, thankfully, he doesn't go for thundering chords but plays the proper notes and just enough of them.

Softly, Bruce paints the picture of "Candy's Room," with "pictures of her heroes

99

on the wall." Pensive with anticipation, he makes his way down the dark hall to Candy and her lips.

They kiss: "My heart's pumpin' to my brain, the blood rushes in my veins, when I touch Candy's lips." Weinberg's playing becomes furious (but never heavyhanded) here and Bruce is beside himself. This is E street eroticism; there's unquenchable energy being directed in the right direction. Candy implores Bruce, "Close your eyes, let them melt, let them fire, let them burn." He is only too obliging.

He's even crazier about Candy than he was about Rosalita on *The E Street Shuffle*. Her numerous other suitors don't faze him, and he'd give "all that I got to give, all that I want, all that I live, to make Candy mine." This is the scorcher of the album, with a truly blazing guitar break by Bruce. It is slight only in length of time, and it's been overlooked because it's a departure from the record's overwhelming preoccupation with angst. But "Candy's Room" is one of the things that makes putting *Darkness on the Edge of Town* on your turntable worthwhile.

Side one is loaded with over twenty-three minutes of music—Bruce has never scrimped on his records and had some difficulty keeping *Darkness* down to ten songs. The closer of the first side is "Racing in the Street," one of the many songs with cars and the road as a milieu, but it is about much more than that.

It commences with a technical description of Bruce's

wheels, but he's kind of somber about it, not nearly as excited as Jan and Dean were when they told us they had a '34 wagon and called it a Woody. The interesting variation about "Racing in the Street" is that it deals with a subject that is loud, swift, and usually exciting, but it is in fact almost a dirge. It has the same "summer's here and the time is right" line as Martha and the Vandellas' "Dancing in the Street" with none of the vivacity.

Despite the boasts about how swift his wheels are and the chronicles of past exploits, it's obvious that the racing life is beginning to feel empty for the narrator of this tune. The memorable time when he "blew that Camaro off my back" in L. A. and ran off with a lovely spectator is now hollow; now "there's wrinkles around my baby's eyes, and she cries herself to sleep at night"; she's got "the eyes of one who hates for just being born."

One wonders exactly what the point is here; on top of the solid organ foundation provided by Danny Federici, Bruce could just be trying to make this sound like a much grander piece of business than we think it is; are we supposed to think these "shut down strangers and hot rod angels" are modern gladiators? And there's the couplet that comes out and grabs you like so many of Springsteen's do: "Some guys they just give up living and start dying little by little, piece by piece." That's a message much bigger than the apparent subject matter of this tune, and it would seem to draw a solid line between those guys and the ones that

Winterland, 1978

100

RICHARD McCAFFREE

go racing in the street.

Still, as Bruce sings this one he sounds tired, hardly fulfilled, not at all as if life is good. Can he be getting too old for this life? Is the blast against the people dying "piece by piece" in there because he's afraid of becoming one of them? "Racing in the Street" has plenty beyond its concern with '69 Chevys and is worth coming back to again and again. Among other things, it's mighty pretty.

With "The Promised Land," side two's opener, Springsteen becomes a bit more worldly; his environment moves well beyond the New Jersey-New York axis and into the Utah desert, and he begins the song with some appropriately western-style harmonica licks. It's still E Street rock, however, and it's not gonna end up on country and western stations.

"The Promised Land" is also the most obviously fictional of Springsteen's songs; he poses himself as the protagonist but we know he did not ever work all day in his daddy's garage in Utah.

This is not one of the major tracks on *Darkness*; the E Street boys actually sound fairly ordinary, thin, and slow, and Clarence's blaring sax solo at midpoint is remarkable chiefly because it makes everything else seem unexceptional. Another take may have been a good idea.

Bruce himself, however, does a bang-up job, and evidence of his continuing development as a vocalist is plentiful in this song. "I ain't a boy, no, I'm a man" is a fervid oath, and the frustrations of work-a-day living become terror from the mouth

of the author-singer:

Sometimes I feel so weak I just want to explode
Explode and tear this town apart
Take a knife and cut this pain from my heart
Find somebody itching for something to start

It may be Utah and not Asbury Park but it's still a cry of someone who's got much more to offer than his surroundings will take. The belief in a promised land is what sustains our hero.

"Factory" is the briefest track on the *Darkness* album but it's a vital piece of biography, a story of young Bruce but mainly a story of his father's sweatshop existence and that of so many men like him; here's a very personal song that is at the same time very universal.

Bruce recites the workday routine over an instrumental backing not very different from "Racing in the Streets." Nothing extraordinary going on here: "it's the working, the working, just the working life."

He sees his father walking through factory gates and he sees the men coming out at day's end "with death in their eyes." It's all very much like the tales Bruce has told interviewers about his young life in New Jersey. And the line "somebody's gonna get hurt tonight" applies to many of the participants, but it would seem to refer specifically to Bruce, who would pay directly for his father's bitterness and frustration. "Factory" is a cut with no excess; Bruce tells his haunting story and gets off. Few,

if any, modern rock writers even tackle this subject matter, especially in as perceptive and sympathetic a manner as Springsteen.

To some critics, "Streets of Fire" is the crux of the fourth album. Bruce sings like a man physically wounded and spiritually battered; his guitar is mean and nasty, a sniper and a viper. He is a wanderer, a loser, displaced and distrustful. Here, the "night's quiet" does not sound peaceful or hospitable.

Lines like "you don't care anymore" and "you realize you wannt let go" could lead you to believe that here is a man so sinned against that he'd as soon pack it in as get up and find out who's at the door. "Streets of Fire," a seeming melting pot for all of Bruce's anguishes, has naturally been seen as a metaphorical treatment of his real life travails. When you hear him say "you realize how they tricked you this time and it's all lies," you can't help but think of the travails that kept him from capitalizing on his full potential at the end of '75.

Like many of the songs on *Darkness on the Edge of Town*, the impact of "Streets of Fire" depends largely on how much you know about the real life Springsteen and how much you cared about him before you put the album on your stereo. It's frightening to hear anyone as downtrodden as Springsteen is on "Streets of Fire," but if you have a little information you can at least understand it. In any case, "Streets" is striking, but to the uninitiated it would be awfully confusing.

"Prove It All Night" has been

called the clinker, the least significant song on *Darkness*. Perhaps not surprisingly, it was the choice for the first single off the album, probably in keeping with the strange but widespread record industry belief that the most meager fare belongs on AM radio.

The fact is that "Prove It All Night" is an enjoyable, unpretentious rocker with some first rate playing by the band, especially Clarence and Springsteen himself. It's another midnight romance involving cars and a girl, but it's more adult, more sober, more realistic, and a bit sadder than anything on, say *The Wild, the Innocent, and the E Street Shuffle*. That, however, was a long five years ago. Bruce has grown up learned a lot and has ingested much that is not good news.

His declaration; "Girl, you want it, you take it, you pay the price" complies with the essential *Darkness on the Edge of Town* dogma that nothing comes easy or without strings attached.

It isn't the rosiest picture Bruce is offering this woman; he admits we all got a hunger for more and we deserve it, and it would be nice if dreams came true. But "this ain't no dream we're living through," and whatever it is, it'll cost ya.

Bruce and the woman are heading somewhere that separates them from the pack, the folks who tell her not to go. To them, Bruce can say "they made their choices and they'll never know, what it means to steal to cheat, to lie, what it's like to live and die." Maybe not, but is that so swell? I guess so; Bruce is one for taking chances, even

if a few of them are misses.

Both he and the woman, whom he neglected to give a name, have got to "prove it all night." The phrase seems to have larger connotations of testing each other's mettle and confidence in each other, but when the album came out jesting young studs were asking each other "did you prove it all night?" The phrase caught on and so does the song; it's one of the few tracks on the record that can be fully appreciated by someone who's never heard Bruce and the E Street Band before.

On *Darkness on the Edge of Town*, Bruce Springsteen often speaks in parables; he deals in much larger lessons than the surface subject matter would suggest. The last chapter of the Gospel According to Springsteen, the title tune, is no exception.

The elements of heroism and romance are here; the former lovers, the woman now living, perhaps not happily, in a grand style and the man still on the other side of the tracks. The third element is the kind of no man's land where they can meet if they choose, the "darkness on the edge of town."

But the bigger matter is Bruce's attempt to settle real matters in his own mind. You can't always keep it bottled up inside; you can't let things eat away and destroy you:

Everybody's got a secret, Sonny,
Something that they just can't face,
Some folks spend their whole lives trying to keep it,
They carry it with them every step that they take.

Till some day they just cut it loose
Cut it loose or let it drag 'em down.

It is Bruce's determination not to be dragged down, and that's something we can applaud. He sings about big, important things that are lost—not exactly the same things as in real life, but the parallel is there—and he swears "them things don't seem to matter much to me now." The "darkness on the edge of town" is a place where there is a second chance for everyone, where every man can have a rebirth.

The analogy is apt; it is almost like a Phoenix that Bruce Springsteen rose up to complete *Darkness on the Edge of Town*. With the negative propaganda that followed, and with the subsequent problems in the studio, even some of his staunchest supporters must have been wondering if they'd ever hear from Bruce again.

So a judgement of the merits of *Darkness on the Edge of Town* involves a few factors not usually present in a musical critique. For one thing, by the time the record was released in June of 1978, we were grateful for *anything* from Bruce.

Secondly, there are the true life tribulations to be considered; their presence is all over this album. One cannot fault Springsteen for making us listen as he pieces things back together again; he intimately shared the joys with us so we should be there for the sorrows. Indeed, no recording artist of Springsteen's stature has ever shown us a larger piece of himself than he

105

JAMES SHIVE

has, and he's someone worth getting a glimpse of.

On straight musical terms *Darkness on the Edge of Town* is only a fair album. The music isn't even showcased that much; live performances have indicated that the E street Band is capable of considerably more than we hear on *Darkness*; they were even shown to better advantage on *Born to Run*.

But what Bruce needed to do was not be a flashy rock idol; he needed to do *this* album, to express these feelings, these disappointments, and, as he does in the final song, resolve to get on with that. And he has done all of that very well. *Darkness* accurately reflects what this chapter of Bruce Springsteen's life is all about.

The pressure, in so many forms, is now off. He is his own man, he is an established giant in the rock field, and he can now do what he wants. The next album will come when he wants it to, assuredly not at another three-year interval. *Darkness on the Edge of Town* has been called a transitional album, and so it is and so it should be. The years 1975 to 1978 were transitional ones for Bruce. He is now in many ways what he always sought to be. How he likes *that*, how he chooses to deal with that is something we will soon learn. For better or worse, there will never be another *Darkness on the Edge of Town*.

The word from the rock critics on *Darkness on the Edge of Town* made it clear that many had not lost faith in Bruce, although they perceived that vast and somewhat surprising changes had oc-

RICHARD McCAFFREE

curred since *Born to Run.*

Jay Cocks, who had written the *Time* cover story, noted t that *Darkness,* in the Top Ten on the album charts, was "lending a little class to that generally tacky neighborhood." Cocks believed the new release "passes the romantic delirium of *Born to Run,* cuts deeper, lingers longer." Although some of the same characters turn up, Cocks felt they were "no longer bursting with the same heady spirit. Here the 'shutdown strangers and hot rod angels' suffer a sudden splintering sense of their own settled fates.

The *Time* writer considered *Darkness* to be "full of gruff courage and sadness, but never despair. He noted "Springsteen reaches high, always making the big grab but never losing aim."

Influential rock critic Dave Marsh heaped praise on Bruce in the review section of *Rolling Stone,* which he edits. He treated the release as an historic occasion. Observing that certain ground breaking efforts "change fundamentally the way we hear rock and roll the way it's recorded, the way it's played," Marsh contended that those are the records that justifiably be "called classics, and I have no doubt that Bruce Springsteen's *Darkness on the Edge of Town* will someday fit as naturally within that list as the Rolling Stone's *Satisfaction* and Sly's *Dance to the Music.*"

Marsh, who felt the album's "dominant instrumental focus" had become Bruce's guitar, said Springsteen had united the best of "L.A. pastoral" with English and Middle American rawness to

become the "only artist I can think of who's simultaneously comparable to Jackson Browne and Peter Townshend."

Peter Knobler, the editor of *Crawdaddy* and a longtime Springsteen booster, underscored the obvious effect of Bruce's legal squabbles on his music. "He lost some incredible amount of money to the lawsuits which kept him out of the recording studio at the very moment he should have been in there documenting his triumphs," contended Knobler. A man who "began as the purest of rock 'n' rollers—he played for the absolute joy and release" but found he had gotten "screwed." It showed, and he was "just now working it out."

To Knobler, one song in particular, "Streets of Fire," showed that Bruce had felt "abandoned, betrayed, he wanders in obvious pain with no relief in sight. His trust is gone ("when you realize how they tricked you this time").

On *Darkness on the Edge of Town,* Knobler perceived "enough raw emotion to make you shake; several songs to take with you to your grave." To him, "the power of Bruce Springsteen has always been that he writes what he knows, and that he's in touch with it, that he makes you feel it too." This trip with Bruce was the most trecherous thus far. "*Darkness on the Edge of Town* leads you unsuspecting into Springsteen's own life and lets you know, want to or not, that, as he says, 'You want it, you take it, you pay the price.'"

Paul Nelson in *Rolling Stone* suggested *Darkness* is about

"the high cost of romantic obsession for adults, not teenagers." He notes, "while the LP offers hope, it's also Springsteen's blackest—though probably best—work."

Nelson noted "Bob Dylan figuratively replaced James Dean, and it's a better-than-even-bet that Bruce Springsteen could succeed both of them."

Time writer Jay Cocks didn't believe Bruce's hiatus had cost him anything from an artistic standpoint. "After almost three years of legal entanglements, a creative time-out and a lingering celebrity hangover, Bruce Springsteen has come storming back, raising a fine ruckus," Cocks saw it, "not just reaffirming his promise as the pre-eminent rock figure of the late '70s, but redeeming, even enhancing it."

Cocks, whose article in '75 was one of the main bases for the hype accusations that beset Springsteen, realized how shallow, ignorant, and inaccurate those claims had been. "Springsteen had to do battle with the crosscurrents of high hopes and deep cynicism that eddied around him," Cocks noted of the period between the third and fourth albums: "There were those who thought his career was a classic case study in media hype. Although most of these critics never listened to his records or saw him in concert, the charge still stung."

As Cocks saw it, Bruce and the E Street Band were better than ever. After a concert, he lauded "the driving delicacy of Roy Bittan's piano, Danny Federici's flights of rough and tumble fantasy on the organ,

and the hang-tough beat of Max Weinberg's drums, Garry Tallent's sinuous serpentine bass lines and the roistering guitar of Miami Steve Van Zandt [which] form the firm foundation. The wailing, extravagant sax solos by Clarence Clemons cut jolting, joking arabesques around the Boss' lead guitar and vocals."

At least one major rock critic was not won over by *Darkness on the Edge of Town.* Jim Miller, writing in *New Times,* argued finally that "the future of rock and roll is not Bruce Springsteen" and

said that at first listening it was hard to believe the album "is as bad as it is."

Miller had some kind words for "Badlands," but suggested "by compressing all his favorite themes of frustration and hope, repression and rebellion, into one emblematic anthem like 'Badlands', Springsteen unwittingly illuminates the strained seriousness and failure of imagination that mars the rest of *Darkness on the Edge of Town.*"

Miller pulled no punches, blasting Springsteen for "plodding band tracks, mush-

mouthed vocals, and an aura of hyped-up hysteria." To the critic, Bruce sounded like "a constipated cowboy drowning in oatmeal" who had produced an album that "is not mature; it's embalmed."

As a gentler addendum, Miller conjectured "if it breaks the spell of high expectations imprisoning him, this debacle may yet enable Springsteen to give himself more of the psychological space he obviously needs to create music that sounds genuinely felt rather than hopelessly contrived. Until then, he will remain a casualty of media canonization, cut loose from the roots that once gave his music immediacy, authority, and an unforced importance."

"This album's stripped down," Springsteen told Robert Duncan, "to run as clean as possible and stay true." He added, *Darkness* is a confrontation with a lot of things. *Born to Run* had a certain romantic feel. This is more realistic."

One difference was that "on *Born to Run* there was the hope of a free ride. On *Darkness,* there ain't no free ride—you wanna ride, you gotta pay. And maybe you'll make it through, but you ain't gonna make it through 'til you been beat, you been hurt, until you been messed up. There's hope, but it's just the hope of, like, survival. It couldn't be a warm, innocent album like *Born to Run* because it ain't that way, it wasn't that way for me any—more. That's why a lot of pain had to be there, because it's real, because it happens."

The protagonists of *Darkness* were different as well. "They're like 28-30 years old, like my age; they're just not kids anymore," their creator observed.

Darkness is about dealing with despair, about people trying to hold on to their dignity in the middle of a hurricane," Springsteen has also explained. "You look around, you see people in the street dug in. You know they're already six feet under, people with nothin' to lose and full of poison. I try to write about the other choice they've got."

Strangely, however, for an album that is so black and negative, Darkness on the Edge of Town has no identifiable villains. "All people do their whole lives is they try to get free, essentially, of all the bullshit that was laid on them coming up," Bruce told Peter Knobler. "You look for someone to blame, something to blame, there is nobody to blame. Nobody specific." That realization is an important one for whatever peace of mind Bruce possesses; it must help keep him from burning up inside, from harboring any huge hatred.

Springsteen sometimes speaks of Darkness on the Edge of Town in cinematic terms. "It's like everybody's always in transit," observed Bruce, who in many ways fits that description. "There's no settling down, no fixed action. You pick up the action, and then at some point— psst!—the camera pans away, and whatever happened, that's what happened. The songs I write, they don't have particular beginnings and they don't have endings. The camera focuses in and then out."

RICHARD McCAFFREE

The cinema has begun to be a big influence on Springsteen the song writer. "That's always how I saw the songs," he explained. "They always had a sort of drive-in quality to them."

For a title for album number four, Springsteen and his manager and co-producer Jon Landau consulted Andrew Sarris' *The American Cinema: Directors and Directions 1929-1968*. Bruce reportedly leaned toward *American Madness* as the working title; Landau favored *History Is Made at Night*.

Springsteen has acknow-

against and fears about larger, unseen, impersonal forces that they cannot touch. "To me, it's like, where do you point the gun?" Bruce wondered. "There's no place to take aim. There's nobody to blame. It's just things, just the way. Whose fault is it? It's a little bit of this guy, a little bit of that guy, a little bit of this other guy. That was real interesting to me . . . And it was great that when the movie came out it was a very popular movie."

One track "Adam Raised a Cain," was reportedly inspired by seeing James Dean in *East of Eden*, a film

Great stories. Actually, what happened was I was thinking of writing that particular song, and I went back trying to get a feeling for it."

Bruce again credits Jon Landau for a vital role in the making of *Darkness on the Edge of Town*. "He helped me see things—to see into things—and somehow it would come out in the songs," Bruce commented. "There's a certain little consciousness barrier [that] gets broken down."

And while a lot of things took time to come to fruition while *Darkness* was being put together, some things went like clockwork. "Streets

"The songs I write, they don't have particular beginnings and they don't have endings. The camera focuses in and then out."

ledged *The Grapes of Wrath* as having influenced the material on *Darkness on the Edge of Town*. He's talking about the movie; he hadn't read the book at the time. "But I've got it in my suitcase," he told Robert Duncan. "I have *got* it."

Bruce was particularly taken by the characters' struggles

about one son who can do no wrong in his father's eyes and another (Dean) who can do no right.

The song was also based on Bruce's Bible reading. "I did read the Bible some," the Boss told Robert Duncan. "I tried to read it for a while about a year ago. It was great. It's fascinating. I got into it quite a ways.

of Fire" and "Something in the Night" were first takes.

To some who don't search very far beneath the surface, *Darkness on the Edge of Town* might have seemed like just another album about cars, the night, and girls. Some have suggested that Bruce was not expanding the scope of his subject matter.

"Everything has its limitations and its ultimate possibilities, and you got to test them to find out what they are," claims Springsteen. "It's like those Italian westerns at the drive-in. I always loved it for me. To be able to go out there tonight means more than it meant three years ago because I had to do a lot to get out there. And like the record meant more than, maybe, the other records."

sibility to the crowd, and that's the most important thing. . . . You can never take it for granted. I feel that very strongly. For the first four years, I had an attitude. I went into every place expect-

> "They always had a sort of drive-in quality about them."

that they showed 'em all at once. That's the way I make these albums—so they get played all at once."

In the film *McCabe and Mrs. Miller*, Warren Beatty played a man of grand vision (if limited practicality) who was so bristling with energy and dreams that he could not sit still. "I've got poetry in me," he'd tell anybody who'd listen.

A similar sense sustained Bruce Springsteen during his dark days of legal entanglements. He spoke as a man with a mission to deliver his own very secular form of street poetry to the people. He knew it was what he was meant to do; he knew that somehow, he would do it.

It was all too good to go to waste, he seemed to feel. In 1978 he explained "the whole band's just too full of life to throw it all away. It makes it much more valuable

Each subsequent record would undoubtedly mean even *more* to the man who set such exacting standards for himself. As Landau commented, "Bruce is determined before he dies to make the greatest rock and roll record ever."

Although he had always established a remarkable rapport and sense of comradeship with his followers, his appreciation of them seemed even greater when he returned for his 1978 concert tour.

In *Rolling Stone*, he talked passionately about those fans. "These people work all week and a lot of times wait in line for ten hours or some incredible amount of time . . . The kid, he's doing his bit. He's forking over his bucks, he's coming down. You've got to make sure he can come down, sit in his seat, and not get blown up. That's your respon-

ing it to be empty. So whoever was there was a big plus. I was glad they were there, and we played our best to whoever was there, always. You just don't lay back in this band, you know. That just don't happen. That's why people come down to see us—because something more is going to happen. Something—just somehow, someway.

"Sometimes after the show the kids'll wait out back and that's the best part," Springsteen continued. "It's like Christmas or something. They don't take it lightly so you have no right to either. It's something that I've never done and never will do. I'll quit before I do that."

The magic between Springsteen and his audience was something the musician considered priceless. "The whole idea is to deliver what money can't pay," he explained.

113

"You don't go out there to deliver $7.50 worth of music. My whole thing is to go out there and deliver what they could not possibly buy."

"I can't go on stage at night and not try and bring it home " he explained in *Creem* to Duncan. "Because . . . what an ingrate??? What a spit in the face of everything that is anything??? I could never do that."

He admitted, "I always sound like some kind of fanatic, some kind of zealot. But I think there's things that people take for granted. How can you take it for granted? I stick too close to the other side to know what's real about this side. And I still got too many people who are close to me who are still living on that other side."

In Houston, Bruce played a three-hour show in the midst of a heatwave of 100 degree days that killed more than twenty people. At intermission Bruce said. "I'm jumping around and there's oceans of sweat coming off my arms and face and all of a sudden . . . no more sweat! I feel my face, bone dry. I guess I got no more. Weird." And that was just intermission!

To say that Bruce reduces the distance between himself and the audience is an understatement In almost every show in 1978, he was leaping down and mingling *with* the audience.

Dave Marsh recounts that in one show, when Bruce was being swarmed over by his passionate followers, an overzealous security guard tried to pull the fans off. Springsteen wouldn't have it. "You guys work here or something?" he asked curtly. "Get outta here. These guys are my friends."

Bruce's appreciation of his fans matches their affection for him. Frequently, on the '78 tour, he would say, "I want to thank all of you for supporting the band for the past three years."

Those who see Springsteen in

Jon Landau, Karen Darbin

114

concert often come away from the experience speaking of the Boss in reventual terms.

"Seeing Springsteen play Boston made me fall in love with rock 'n' roll all over again," Paul Nelson wrote in *Rolling Stone* during the '78

DAVID GAHR

tour. "Here's this guy who just spent a year breaking his back on a new album, who'd gone straight into a four-month tour, and you couldn't pay him enough not to play for almost three hours. Every night. No matter where. Or to whom."

Nelson noticed, "Springsteen has carefully cultivated the Method actor's idiosyncratic timing, added a professional street character's sense of the dramatic, a dancer's knack for picturesque tableau, and wrapped the whole package in explosive vulnerability and the practiced pose of a tender, punky hood."

Bruce knows how he'll pace a show, and he knows he won't leave anything out. When requests come from the audience, he answers good-naturedly but emphatically, "don't rush me, don't rush me."

And Bruce is nothing if not persistent; he'll stay up there until he gets it right. On one occasion he exclaimed, "I'm not going to give up until there are people dying in their seats."

Unlike many rock stars, Bruce wouldn't think of showing up on stage "under the influence." He has called being drugged for a concert "like coming on stage on crutches."

"I think, for most musicians, it has to be like life or death or else it's not worth it," Springsteen contends. "That's why every night we play a real long time, and we play real hard. I want to be able to go home and say I went all the way tonight—and then I went a little further."

"My whole life, I was always around a lot of people whose lives consisted of just this compromising," Spring-

115

steen has noted. "They knew no other way—that's where rock 'n' roll was important because it said there could be."

Bruce is wary of concert security guards and their insensitivity to fans. "What happens is that a lot of the security in a lot of places don't understand," Bruce said to Robert Duncan. "Kids get real excited, but they're not *mean,* they're just excited."

Springsteen has even been known to go into the audience and separate fans from guards. Recalling one such incident, he said "this kid's not looking for trouble. What happens is the kids have a reaction to security, which is if the security guard grabs 'em, they think they're gonna get thrown out of the show." Bruce explains, "I can't watch kids getting knocked down in the front row because that's me. That's a part of me."

Springsteen does everything humanly possible to insure the highest quality in his concerts. On the 1978 tour, the meticulous Boss was apparently so concerned about the quality of sound that he would sit in every part of a hall and listen, ordering changes in the mix if anything at all was less than superlative.

The long stretch of one-nighters apparently doesn't bother Bruce. "Home never had a big attraction for me," he revealed in *Creem.* "I get excited staying in all these different hotels, in a whole lot of rooms. I'm always curious what the wallpaper's gonna be like. Do I have a big bed or a little one? And what's this funny painting?"

Most of all, New Jersey's number one rock and roller

seems happiest that he has been able to break free of the norm in this life, to avoid the fates that seem to greet so many citizens.

"You grow up, and they bury you," Bruce surmised in a *Creem* interview with Robert Duncan. "They keep throwing dirt on you, throwing dirt on and dirt on and dirt on, and some guys they bury so deep they never get out. Six foot, twelve foot down. Other guys, something comes along and they're able to get some of it away. They get a hand free or they get free one way or another.

"I don't think you ever really blow it all off, but the idea is to keep charging. It's like anything. Everybody can't make it. You can see the guys on the street who aren't going to make it, and that's a frightening thing.

"That's what I'm talking about," Bruce continued. "That some people get dug in so deep that there's a point where it stops getting on them and they roll over, start digging down. Because they don't know which way is up. You get down so deep that you don't know which way's up. You don't know if you're digging sideways, up, down, you don't *know* . . . until something comes along, if you're lucky, and shakes you 'til all of a sudden you have a certain sense of direction and at least know where you're going.

"A lot of people don't ever get that. You go into bars and you see the guys wandering around in there who got the crazy eyes. They just *hate.* They're just looking for an immediate expenditure of all this build-up. They're just

screaming to throw it all off. But you can't and it turns into, like, death throes. A guy walks into a bar, a little guy, and he walks up to another guy, a *dome,* and the little guy's looking to get *creamed.* Looking to get massacred. He *wants* to. 'Look', he's saying, 'I'm dying here and I don't know what the fuck to do'. It's a scary thing when you see the guys that ain't gonna get out, just ain't gonna get out. "You just see too many faces," concluded Bruce. "It's the kind of thing where you can't save everybody, but you gotta try."

He does try, and he succeeds plenty of the time, but he gets a bit embarrassed by excessive praise. The plaudits from the two Los Angeles dailies were effusive, and Bruce told Dave Marsh jokingly, "See all that fancy stuff in the papers about me? Big deal, huh? I gotta tell you, I only levitate to the upper deck on Wednesdays and Fridays . . . Wednesdays and Fridays and I don't do no windows."

Bruce has yet to appear on any of the TV rock shows; his first appearance of any kind was a news interview with KABC in Los Angeles in July of last year.

But he keeps busy. After his major summer tour, Bruce embarked on a November and December tour of colleges, many of them in the midwest. He dropped in on other folks' albums—he can be heard counting off "one, two, three, four" on a track by The Dictators and on Lou Reed's "Street Hassle," Springsteen can at one point be heard in the background crooning, "Baby we were

116

RICHARD McCAFFREE

born to run."

The rest of the gang had plans, too. Ian Hunter, former leader of Mott the Hoople and colleague of David Bowie and Mick Ronson, let it be known in November that he was making a recording and concert return with a lineup that would include three E Stret Band members. Roy Bittan, Garry Tallent, and Max Weinberg would work their schedules around Springsteen's plans so they could aid Hunter's comeback.

In the meantime, Bruce is electrifying audiences with his live performances, often embellishing the originals. "Prove It All Night" becomes a powerhouse number in concert, with a two-minute introduction of foreboding piano and screeching guitar. The album version seems a mere shell for the E Street boys to augment.

"Jungleland" becomes "a real death waltz," almost heralding the arrival of the Apocalypse. In "Badlands," when Bruce shrieks from his soul, "I believe in the love," you know he believes.

We've already been given more than a few glimpses of what we can expect from the next Bruce Springsteen album or two. Word has it that between the releases of *Born to Run* and *Darkness on the Edge of Town,* Bruce authored at least thirty songs, and part of the delay on the latter album was caused by indecision concerning which of many possible selections should be included.

Several new songs not on *Darkness* were part of Springsteen's 1978 concert repertoire; some of them are ex-

pected to be on the next studio album and even more could be on the always promised live set.

For starters, there are Bruce's own versions of "Because the Night" and "Fire." Bruce diehards immediately will insist that his version of "Because the Night" beats Patti Smith's hands down, but that seems a knee-jerk reaction. There's no need to compare the two and no basis, really. For one thing, it was a writing collaboration, which indicates cooperation, not competition. More than that, however, one should keep in mind that Patti's singing "hold me close, try and understand" means different things to different people than Bruce's mouthing the same lyrics.

"Fire" is quite a bit better in the hands of Bruce, however. Robert Gordon's rendering was a bit limited by his stylized Elvis posturing. On "Fire" Bruce is more stealthy, creepy, and lethal, more suited to the matter on which he speaks. And the E Street Band does a nice job of underscoring the Boss' dastardliness here.

At the end of 1978, in an effort to broaden their appeal, The Pointer Sisters recorded an album of mainstream rockers produced by Richard Perry. "Fire" was among the selections; their version broke no new ground. Nevertheless. it became a huge Top 40 hit for the siblings.

There's also plenty of material at hand that hasn't been recorded by anyone yet. "Rendezvous," another song with that "wall of sound" feel, has been in and out of his concert lineup since 1976.

"The Promise" also dates back that far; emotionally, it is the equivalent of primal scream therapy, an exorcizing of Bruce's own demons. Written in reaction to his falling out with Mike Appel, it includes the lyrics "I built that challenger by myself, but I needed money, so I sold it/I lived a secret I should have kept to myself, but I got drunk one night and I told it." He sounds a little bitter and betrayed, at the very least. When getting ready to release *Darkness on the Edge of Town,* at a time when his non-musical problems were still fresh in everyone's mind, Bruce showed appropriate restraint by keeping the song off the album.

Springsteen would refer to "The Promise" as "my peace with the past" while also proclaiming that his legal imbroglios were given too much credit for influencing his work. "I wrote it before there was a lawsuit," he told Paul Nelson in a discussion of the song. "I don't write songs about lawsuits."

Perhaps in reaction to suggestions that "The Promise" was a thinly veiled account of the Appel dispute, Bruce returned to the studio and added an extra verse with a meaning that is clearly more universal.

"Point Blank" was included in many of the 1978 concerts, and it is one of Springsteen's scariest, most harrowing songs. It begins with Roy Bittan's trickling, sneaking piano and a subdued Bruce, who reaches more feverish peaks as the song progresses.

Bruce is singing to a young woman, advising "they shot you point blank . . . you didn't

119

fool this town, little girl, that's the facts . . . they've got you in their sights, one false move and baby the lights go out."

The genuinely disturbing song also predicts "all your hopes and your promises, somehow they just fade away" and warns "but don't you know, little darling, nothing survives."

Negative it is, pessimistic, too, and obviously written in one of the author's darker moods. Throughout he is dealing with large, amorphous, unseen enemies, the proverbial "they" who just won't let things be the way you innocently would wish them to be. And although he is singing as a wise and tested man presenting the facts to an inexperienced female, the overwhelming impression remains that he is really singing to himself, that the words are for his benefit. "They" are folks who've beset Bruce at many a turn; he sings with a pain that is certainly his own.

In concert doing "Independence Day," Bruce once supplied a preface. "I dedicate this to my father. I tease him a lot, but he was always telling me, 'You should be better than me, whatever you do.'"

"Independence Day" has been well-received by concert goers, praised by critics, and pegged for the next album. It would have been on *Darkness on the Edge of Town* if Bruce didn't feel that one song on tortured father-son relationships—he already had "Adam Raised a Cain"—was sufficient for one album.

That's his prerogative, of course, but the fact is that "Independence Day" is the better of the two by no small

120

Patti Smith and Bruce

121

Robert Gordon, Bruce and Link Wray

measure. As fine as the *Dark-ness* tracks are, "Independence Day" might have been the most emotionally effective of the lot.

After Bittan's slow piano opening (he seems to be carrying more and more of the instrumental load in recent days), Bruce recounts a family relationship that has already broken down. "No talking gonna change anything now, we won't change this thing even if we could somehow."

Then, as if he sees what he speaks of hovering over the stage, like Macbeth and the ghost of his father, Bruce gasps "there's a darkness in this house that's got the best of us, there's a darkness in this town that's got us too." But he swears "they can't touch me now and you can't touch me now." The message is "so say goodbye, it's Independence Day, all men must make their way come Independence Day."

There's so much to purge, so the song goes on. "I don't know what it always was with us, we chose the words and yeah we chose the lines, there was just no way this house could hold the two of us." At this point Clarence's saxophone actually cries, weeping not nearly so gently as an ex-Beatle's guitar.

The prognosis remains bleak. Bruce reaffirms "nothing we can say is gonna change anything now," and that things are moving far too fast for the two of them to keep pace with. "Pretty soon everything we've known will be just swept away," notes a resigned Bruce.

This is a long, insistent ballad; the music is sparse while the lyrics are given emphasis. This is truly wrenching stuff, perhaps a whole album's worth of pathos. The song is so strong that it deserves to be a centerpiece of the next one; it may be the most telling father-son tale ever set to rock music.

John Milward saw much of this material performed at Northwestern University, and in *Downbeat* he saw Springsteen as "an example of how a vibrant artist can transcend the heavyhandedness of the music industry in which he works." To Milward, "his concerts always evoke the passion, power, and vulnerability of the best rock and roll."

At Northwestern, Bruce opened with Buddy Holly's "Rave On"; Milward also saw vestiges of Elvis, the Yardbirds, Dylan, Bo Diddley, and the Animals in the repertoire, but noted, "Springsteen doesn't clone these musicians, but rekindles them in himself." The praise for the band was effusive. "Each of the E Streeters is perfectly woven into the musical framework," wrote Milward, who saw the band as "the true vehicle of Springsteen's rock dreams."

There were even more songs left over from Bruce's fertile writing period, and he tossed a few to Southside Johnny, whose *Hearts of Stone* emerged shortly after *Darkness*. There were other E Street touches to Johnny's record; Steve Van Zandt produced, arranged, wrote some tunes, and played guitar, while Max Weinberg handled drums in his mighty fashion. Johnny and Bruce are old buddies, and Bruce has also composed tunes on the first two Asbury Jukes albums.

Bruce, Van Zandt, and Johnny Lyon collaborated on "Trapped Again," a song with obvious debts to Motown; it could be sung by Diana Ross. It's another "baby can't you understand what I'm going through" variation, but a fine one. Springsteen also wrote "Talk to Me," a straight ahead rocker, and the title song "Hearts of Stone." The latter deals with an impossible love relationship; it is a poignant ballad that concludes "nothing good ever lasts."

Springsteen's *Darkness* tour ended on New Year's 1979. In addition, he appeared again that year for two special nights in September. One of the major events of 1979 was the "No Nukes" series of concerts at New York's Madison Square Garden. The benefits were sponsored by the antinuclear Musicians United For Safe Energy (MUSE), a group led by Jackson Browne, Graham Nash, John Hall, and Bonnie Raitt.

The extraordinary "No Nukes" lineup featured those four plus The Doobie Brothers, James Taylor, Carly Simon, Tom Petty, Crosby, Stills, and Nash, Ry Cooder, Poco, Gil Scott-Heron, and Ray Parker, Jr. And as big as the news of the concerts themselves was the announcement that Bruce Springsteen and the E Street Band would be on the bill. At this stage, Bruce probably could have sold out the Garden three hundred sixty-five nights a year.

Bruce had never been known for being overtly political, but here he contributed what he could—his own music for a worthy cause. When the three-record set of concert performances was released, it included material Bruce didn't write but did love performing.

He did a very bouncy version of Maurice Williams' "Stay," sharing vocals with Jackson Browne and Rosemary Butler (with Clarence doing the comically deep bass part). Federici led the band with his jaunty organ until Clarence assumed control with a churning gutbucket sax solo.

"Stay" segued into one of Bruce's concert staples, the "Devil with the Blue Dress Medley." Some of the material was originally done by Little Richard but had been more recently recreated by '60s star Mitch Ryder, a give-it-all-you've-got dynamo whose spirit might have been reincarnated in Springsteen. The opening chords by Federici lead into "Devil with the Blue Dress," "Good Golly, Miss Molly," and "Jenny Take a Ride," all delivered in rollicking, bar-band style.

Springsteen and Tom Petty were the only headliners not to make a statement on the program notes to the "No Nukes" album, but Bruce's feelings are clear. "Roulette," a song he wrote about Three Mile Island, is truly harrowing, though at this stage it may never be on an album.

Between the end of the 1978 tour and the "No Nukes" appearances, much time and energy was devoted to songwriting, a feverish output that would result in a double album in 1980.

By this time, fans knew there were certain things they could always rely upon from a Springsteen composition. The first lines always immediately established a character or a sense of place, whereas the typical rock lyric caused a listener to visualize nothing at all. And while many rock songs are cold and elicit almost no emotional response (hell, they don't even seem like the work of human beings), Bruce is consistently affectionate or at least respectful to the people he writes about.

All of this was again evident with 1980's *The River,* the long-awaited fifth album. In many ways, it was a more "mature" effort for Bruce. The subject of marriage and commitment and involvement hadn't been a large part of his work until now. Of course, there had always been songs with women in them and he wrote of romance, but the complicated issues of give-and-take relationships appeared more often in Springsteen's songs when he neared and then passed thirty. That's often when complexities become apparent, when determining the parameters of a relationship can become a tiring full-time job.

The four-sided, 20-song *The River* was produced by Springsteen, Jon Landau, and Van Zandt. The cover photo of Bruce in a work shirt and drowsy look is by Frank Stefanko, who had done the *Darkness* cover. The album was recorded at The Power Station in New York and mixed at Clover Recording Studios in Los Angeles.

The River's first side commences with four rockers. "The Ties That Bind" features a clanging guitar (perhaps a 12-string) and a blaring solo by Clarence. The woman of this tale has been hurt and wants to walk her own path alone, but Bruce warns her there are bonds she can't ignore. "Sherry Darling" is an old-style bit of comic celebration suited to Gary "U.S." Bonds in his heyday. It's very funny, a "three's a crowd" yarn about riding in a car

with a darling girlfriend and her very unwelcome mother. We may be forgiven for laughing as Bruce's patience with Ma wears thin. The verses have organ as their main musical underpinning, but as befits a song of this genre, Clarence again gets a chance to wail.

"Jackson Cage" truly seethes; the music has the sound of a struggle to break the chains the characters metaphorically wear. The "cage" is the claustrophobic place these people call home. It's tough, grimy, gritty, steamy, anonymous, and hopeless. It's hard to escape in your own mind what your fate is. A man may dream of something better, but with morning returns the reality—that the cage is a heartless, dehumanizing place. This is the first of many songs on the album telling of characters whose destiny is beyond their control.

"Two Hearts" is next, completing a seamless quartet, almost a medley. The song warns that a decision to go it alone in this world is the wrong choice (much the same theme as "The Ties That Bind"). Even if you've been disappointed in love, "two hearts are better than one." And tough as it may be to find the compatible heart, Bruce promises to keep on searching.

The coda to side one is one of Springsteen's major opuses, "Independence Day." The performance is much as it had been in the shows on the *Darkness* tour, except that in place of Bittan's piano is an organ that resembles a carnival calliope—a touch that makes this summation of a father-son relationship even

more wistful. There is both a sad empathy and a proud vow in Bruce's promise to his father: he'll not be beaten down like his father was. The tragic irony of this embattled relationship is that it may have been generated because, as the singer notes, the father and son are so alike. Springsteen fanatics had tapes of this song from radio concerts, but it's fortunate that such a classic is here on *The River* to endure.

Much of the album is just pure entertainment, and that holds true for "Hungry Heart," *The River's* first single and side two's opener. It's buoyant and very contagious, and has a chorus (with backing vocals by ex-Turtles Mark Volman and Howard Kaylan) that a mass audience can grab a hold of. The restlessness and emotional longing Bruce writes of here are also fit themes for airplay. "Hungry Heart" would reach number one, even though Bruce had expressed doubts about putting it on *The River* but did so at Landau's urging.

While the opening songs on the first two sides each deal with romantic complications, the second tracks are joyous. "Out in the Street," like "Sherry Darling," is simply a good time, while it simultaneously reiterates Bruce's empathy for the working folk. The hero and his girl are hardworking types who just can't wait for that Friday bell to ring so they can escape to the pavement. Here, the hero feels totally at home and completely free, and the lyrics detail endless permutations of that ecstasy.

"Crush on You" is a solid little rocker, one of the songs on which we are most aware of Garry Tallent's nimble bass foundation. A particularly raspy-voiced Bruce, who is of course singing in a state of excitement, confesses that he is so smitten with a pretty woman he sees that his heart takes precedence over his brain. He loses all reason, but that's understandable if the woman is everything he claims (he compares her to the Venus de Milo and Sheena of the Jungle). This is what it sounds like to sing with your libido out of control.

The fourth straight hard rocker is the riproaringest of all, "You Can Look (But You Better Not Touch)." It's a comic piece about a sad sack whose material and hormonal desires are never quite fully realized; alas, he is confined to looking. "You Can Look" is highlighted by a sizzling and tasty guitar solo by Mr. Springsteen.

"I Wanna Marry You" alters the prevailing mood. It's real Italian troubadour stuff, replete with very schmaltzy organ. Yet this song contains much of what fans love most about Springsteen. He has sweet feelings for the characters in this playlet, people who must come to realize that the failure of one's highest expectations isn't necessarily a tragedy. The singer has watched, week after week, a young woman pushing a baby carriage down the street. She's a single mother of two (this is a very contemporary situation), and Bruce suggests it must be tough for her to work and handle all these responsibilities alone. Although it seems they've never spoken, he recommends tying the knot. They aren't Romeo and Juliet,

they're adults and, he suggests, should be realists. He can't magically provide the stuff of her dreams, but he can help quite a bit: that's as much as he'll promise. But it sounds like the most honest offer she'll get, and an advantageous arrangement for the two of them. The appeal of "I Wanna Marry You" is its sweet frankness, vintage Springsteen. Among other things, he's a believer in second chances.

That song's juxtaposition with the title track, which follows, is a neat bit of irony, because in "The River" there *are* no second chances. With its acoustic guitar and harmonica opening, it could be a "prequel" to a record Bruce would release in 1982.

The hero of "The River" comes from a place where a man is brought up just like the generation before him. Still, his beginnings seem promising enough. He has his sweetheart Mary, and he has the river, a place where they go together and everything seems right. The light cascading of Roy Bittan's piano and Max's flickering drumbeats bring us *all* down to the river.

Unfortunately, the hero's future is over before he gets to it. Mary gets pregnant and they have a wedding thoroughly devoid of romance, frills, or niceties at the courthouse. The hero gets a construction job, but a stagnant economy puts an end to that. What was so important to him as a teenager is now so distant and unattainable it's not even an echo; he can hardly remember what it was. And, of course, the marriage sours.

He can still remember the good old days riding with this

lovely girl, lying on the riverbanks, where he would hold her close to feel the life within her. But when Bruce sings that he is haunted by such recollections, it's in a tortured voice that gives us shivers. And, as he learns at the end, even the river has dried up.

At his best, when the material demands it, Springsteen can interpret a song with all the impact of a classical actor's dramatic reading. He created this material and he feels it, of course, but many artists can't deliver their own goods as effectively as Bruce does. His voice makes this saga of a life of nightmarish dead ends into a true tragedy.

It's the title track, and these are themes key to the whole record. Bruce composed much of this material when this country, following a generation in which the overall picture looked rosy, was experiencing some of the worst times it had gone through since the Depression, particularly in the blue-collar segment of the population. This is a Dickensian working class tragedy, the kind of thing that has solidified Springsteen's reputation as an artist with a heart as big as his talent.

"Point Blank," which opens side three, has essentially the same arrangement it had during the *Darkness* concerts, although a few lyrics have been altered. It remains a riveting tale of lost hope. The woman Bruce addresses has passively taken what life handed her, which wasn't much. The promises of a good life seem gone: the next arrival won't be a romantic hero, it'll be a welfare check. Bruce feels loss, too. He dreams of a great time he had with her in a favorite club, but the reality is that she shows no recognition when he sees her in the street.

There actually is a Cadillac Ranch out in Texas; the landowner purchased a fleet of old Caddies and *planted* them in the ground, with their front hoods underground and their rear trunks to the sky (it's all depicted on the lyric sheet). Bruce's "Cadillac Ranch" is one of the most popular and best rockers on *The River.* It's propelled by the jaunty Federici organ (reminiscent again of the old Gary Bonds sound) and great Springsteen guitar rambles; the performance is 100 percent celebration.

Check out the words, though, and it's a pretty enigmatic number. It's another cars-and-girls song, but it's got a twist. The singer describes the Caddies in beautifully descriptive terms, and you think he's in love with the car, but all of this is interspersed with imagery of final destinations and last voyages. On close inspection, this is a wonderfully raucous tune about driving to a cemetery in a hearse.

"I'm a Rocker" follows at an even quicker tempo on a repeating piano riff and loads of handclaps. The imagery here is all superhero stuff; the "rocker" invokes the identities of James Bond, Batman, Kojak, and other pop heroes but constantly reassures his "baby" that if she's in "crisis" or "disaster"—mainly the heartbreaking romantic kind—that he's the only man for the rescue mission. It's a clever, humorous conceit. And it shows how facile the

craft of songwriting has become for Bruce.

"Fade Away," which became a single, slows things down. It's another troubadour number; listening to Danny Federici play, you don't have to be told he's Italian. The only other singer who could put this across is probably Willy DeVille, but this is only one of the genres the versatile Bruce operates within. Here is the flip side of the swaggering chap of "I'm a Rocker." Here, our man has been dumped in favor of another guy and can't accept the loss. He can't give it up; he doesn't want to fade away. The pain of romantic distress is etched all over Bruce's voice. The very real heartbreak of lost romance is here; the singer can't accept being a vague memory or passing acquaintance to his lost love. What "Fade Away" captures, as well as any Springsteen number, is that above all else, lost love can be absolutely terrifying.

"Stolen Car" is a wonderful closer to side three, coming after "Fade Away." Musically, it's soft and simple enough to be an outtake from the yet-to-be-heard *Nebraska.* We've seen romance in various stages on this side of *The River,* but on "Stolen Car" we get the entire picture—the early, innocent, giddy promise and then the drifting apart for reasons not simple to explain.

The rudimentary musical elements—the bottom-heavy acoustic guitar and twinkling piano giving way to a somber organ and a dirgelike chorus—make "Stolen Car" a haunting, even spooky number. Bruce captures the numbness that comes with

the *incomprehensibility* of such loss, a loss so perplexing but so total. The hero drives around in a stolen car, wondering when he'll get caught and feeling so completely adrift that he might just vaporize into thin air.

"Fade Away" and "Stolen Car" aren't sets of platitudes, nor sorry clichés. These are songs of hurt that *really* hurt. Bruce's fans know that whatever subject he tackles seems so genuine. This isn't pathos; it's angst.

We really need a change of pace now, and "Ramrod," side four's opener, is it. Bruce has indicated in interviews, lest anyone misunderstand, that he is mocking the bragging stud of this track. "Ramrod" is a musical cousin of "I'm a Rocker," with the same buoyant organ, insistent thumping bass, and a gutty sax solo. If this is satire, it's affectionate, because the hero's just the kind of guy Springsteen feels for—a hardworking son of a gun who's got plenty of steam to blow. There are abundant double entendres here. The upshot is that after a few verses of describing what he can do, the guy, out of decency or desperation, proposes *marriage* in his own crude vernacular. As we well know by now, circumstances and attitudes can run the gamut in the course of a Springsteen tune.

The 12-string guitar and piano opening of "The Price You Pay" are reminiscent of "The Promised Land," and there's a short instrumental break in the middle that seems culled from that song. On the whole, however, this song is a bit softer and slower, with more of an air of resignation. This isn't the promised land; hope *doesn't* spring eternal.

"The Price You Pay" is a strange, disturbing song, in some ways cryptic. In every situation, for every person, there seems to be a "price" exacted for whatever choice we make or path we take. Anywhere we go, anything we do, is bound to have some hurting consequences. As the song goes on, it's hard to tell where Bruce is going with this idea until the last couple of lines, in which he rebels against the whole idea of paying that price. After singing for almost five minutes in a listlessly melancholy tone, he spits the last line out in a rage, rebelling against the idea of paying. The idea of a "price" is universal; it never becomes specific here. But it's huge. And the shift in mood in that very last line is real drama, truly chilling.

"Drive All Night" is an ambling, lazy, way-past-midnight tune, sort of like "Racing in the Street" on *Darkness*. It's slowly intoxicating and, like "Stolen Car," it contemplates romantic loss from behind the wheel of an automobile. Again Bruce gives us a vivid sense of the physical pain of a sundered relationship: on a sweltering night, the hero's wish is just to have and hold this woman.

With his fascination for the road and feeling for the working man, this guy who drives all night may do it professionally—as a trucker. But that doesn't really matter; what he's saying is he will go to great lengths to get back what was dear to him. It appears, as the verses unfold, that his message is getting through to the woman.

Bruce's impression of Frank Gorshin impersonating Burt Lancaster

"Drive All Night," at 8:26 the album's longest track, is an occasion for Max's very delicate drumming, Danny's lush, enveloping organ, and one of the richest sax solos Clarence has on the four sides. It also contains Bruce's most imploring vocalizing. This tormented lover doesn't keep anything close to his vest; his anguished voice conveys every bit of the heartache he feels. There is no-holds-barred emotion in Bruce's singing of the final verse. This is another Springsteen song that builds in intensity from start to finish.

"Drive All Night" would be a logical capper to *The River*, but there's one more song, a lilting, almost countrified track with celestial keyboards behind it. The sound of "Wreck on the Highway" belies the content. Actually, it seems like a very bad dream. The singer, on a deserted road, comes upon a grisly crash site in the rain, and there, by himself, he's confronted by the wounded victim, imploring him for help.

He imagines the young man's lover getting the bad news, and back home, he watches his own lover sleep, holds her tight, and can't get that wreck out of his mind. For one reason or another, we've all had those late-night moments where we stare and watch our slumbering mate, realizing how devastating the loss of that person would be. It is somehow a reality that's more vivid in these quiet moments.

So, Bruce has closed *The River* with a note of universal impact. And he's turned a narrative of someone else's accident into another personal story of loss. "Wreck on the Highway" is an epilogue to "Drive All Night": you could imagine either that the dead driver was the protagonist of the earlier tune or that the guy *witnessing* this accident is that same fellow, still driving all night and finally being reunited with his darling. In any case, the song continues the motif of loss, of paying prices, of not getting through unscathed.

The River was something very different for Springsteen fans to digest. Some of the sounds were familiar, as on "The Price You Pay" and "Drive All Night." There was also some memorably serious material, songs like "Independence Day" and "Point Blank," in which the strength of the lyric writing overshadowed the spare musical settings. Songs like "The River" and "Stolen Car" proved Bruce's maturation as a composer. And there was plenty of unadorned rock and roll—so much so that, for the first time, we had a Springsteen album in which not every track had a personality and flavor all its own. The rockers, except for a standout like "Cadillac Ranch," tended to blur together. That's not really a criticism. When you have twenty songs to listen to, you're not likely to consider each one distinctive. *The River* is a mammoth achievement, and it was an important step in expanding Bruce's audience to the size worthy of a superstar. Yet in this wealth of material, some songs drift from memory. It might be easy to remember every song on *Born in the U.S.A.*, but only the most fanatic Springsteen addicts could name all twenty songs on *The River*.

In *Rolling Stone*, Paul Nelson declared that Bruce's lyrics were "filled with an uncommon sense and intelligence that could only have come from an exceptionally warmhearted but wary graduate of the street of hard knocks." Like other reviewers, Nelson cautioned listeners to consider the album as a whole. To him, "scope, context, sequencing and mood are everything here." He suggested that "complete immersion is called for. Each song is just a drop in the bucket."

In this "epic exploration of the second acts of American lives," Nelson felt Springsteen "has lost some of his naturalness and seemed more than a bit self-conscious about being an artist." Personally, Nelson preferred "the innocent zest and relative openness of *Born to Run*." Still, the review was generally laudatory, even if he concluded, "Though I consider *The River* a rock 'n' roll milestone, in a way I hope it's also Independence Day."

Surmising the reception given to *The River*, Brock Helander wrote in *The Rock Who's Who* that it had been acclaimed not only as best album of the year but of the last several years.

In the *Rolling Stone* 1980 Reader's Poll, Bruce and *The River* were undefeated. Springsteen was Artist of the Year, the E Street gang was Band of the Year, *The River* earned Album of the Year honors, and "Hungry Heart" was voted Single of the Year. Bruce was also picked as top vocalist and top songwriter, while Jon Landau led the producer ranks. In the instrumentalist category, Clarence was second to guitar legend Jeff Beck.

The wealth of material on *The River* demonstrated someting fans probably already knew; Bruce is one of the most prolific rock composers. Meticulous attention to production detail and decisions about song selection may be reasons for the long gaps between albums, but a dearth of material is certainly not a factor.

Indeed, something *was* left over, and the flip sides of two singles from *The River* were not on the album. The B side of "Hungry Heart" was a red-hot riff called "Held Up Without a Gun," a swift shouter that almost sets the turntable

afire in 1:15.

The flip side of "Fade Away," "Be True," deserved a better fate. It's among Bruce's best from the period, it certainly belongs on an album, and it's managed a high level of popularity for a recording that's hard to come by.

"Be True" grabs our attention in the opening couplet, as Bruce tells a dreamy young woman not to place him in with "all your leading men." Her expectations of romance seem to be motion picture fantasies, and her real-life affairs are a trail of broken promises and disappointments. For his part, Bruce vows to be different from the guys who've told her

appealing lies. His suggestion is that they be true—true to life, and true to each other.

The track gains momentum as it moves on, and it contains one of Max Weinberg's finest lessons in how to be a rock drummer. Seeming to possess the limbs of many men, he nimbly provides an extra layer of urgency to the brief soaring saxophone solo that wraps up a very exciting song.

The tour accompanying *The River*'s release would last from October 1980 to June of 1981. Due to ever increasing ticket demands, it had to be in bigger halls (some satisfying experiences in larger arenas had caused Bruce to abandon his earlier misgiv-

The E Street front line of Clarence, Bruce, Garry, and Steve during 1980 tour

ings about such places). The E Street crew had been away from the concert scene for nearly two years, but the public hadn't forgotten them. In several midwestern cities, ticket sales quadrupled previous totals. The number of requests at Madison Square Garden reportedly could have filled that venue for sixteen nights. The tour, said *Rolling Stone* writer Fred Schruers, "gives ample life to his performing legend" and "overcomes the stigma of being an East Coast phenomenon."

The listening public knew what a special performer Bruce was. Midwest concert promoter Cal Levy noted that the audiences included "salesmen, lawyers, a very *clean* crowd." Indeed, people who had long ago stopped going to rock concerts were still going to watch Bruce. To Schruers, Springsteen "may indeed be one of the few authentic rockers still celebrated by the aging gentry who fueled the '60s rock-and-roll explosion."

Bruce always gave them what they came for, making every show count and explaining, "I keep in mind you only have one chance." As he told Schruers, "Some guy bought his ticket, and there's a promise made between the musician and the audience. When they support each other, that's a special thing. It goes real deep, and most people take it too lightly."

The tour kicked off in Ann Arbor, Michigan, where hometown boy Bob Seger joined Bruce onstage for a duet on "Thunder Road." Later, in Los Angeles, Bruce dueted with Jackson Browne on "Sweet Little Sixteen."

The first night of that four-night Los Angeles stand was a benefit for Vietnam Veterans, and comments made by Bruce onstage became the basis for a radio campaign. He was typically eloquent in uncomplicated language: "It's like when you're walking down a dark street at night, and out of the corner of your eye you see somebody getting hurt in a dark alley, but you keep walking on because you think it don't have nothing to do with you and you want to get home. Vietnam turned this whole country into that dark street, and unless we walk down those dark alleys and look into the eyes of those men and women, we are never gonna get home."

In Canada's *MacLean's*, Bart Testa was impressed by the reaction Bruce's ballads were receiving in concert; he would often stand stock-still through four of the softer tunes, and "his voice was a confident instrument."

Testa noted that Bruce's arrival as a more than regional star had come despite his violation of the music business' cardinal rules. "By taking another two years to release *The River* . . . he threw away whatever momentum he had gained, perversely courting disaster all over again," noted Testa.

To Testa, Springsteen, soaked in linament and massaged to restore his equilibrium after another grueling show, "looked exactly like a featherweight boxer and not like a songwriter at all" at a post-concert bash in the bowling alleys beneath Madison Square Garden. Testa carried the sports motif even further, saying "The rock persona Springsteen has taken on is

close to the ethnic fighters of another generation. He is rock's Rocky, a kid with big ambitions from the crummy part of town."

The E Streeters were in Philadelphia when John Lennon was murdered, and there was doubt as to whether they should go on at the Spectrum the following night. There was no question for Bruce, however, who thought they had the same job to do as Lennon had had. Lennon, of course, had been an inspiration, and Bruce told the Philly crowd that both he and many of them wouldn't have been in that spot at that time if not for Lennon. "It's a hard world that makes you live with a lot of things that are unlivable," he said. "And it's hard to come out here and play tonight, but there's nothing else to do."

By 1981, Bruce had also conquered Europe. The tour was a sold out triumph in several countries, and the record was a smash everywhere Bruce performed. In Britain, *The River* reached number two and was on the charts a full 52 weeks.

The Bruce of the early '80s— the adult who had triumphed over so many obstacles—was someone to learn a lesson from. To Fred Schruers, Bruce was a man wanting to "inspire by example—the example of a trashed and resurrected American spirit."

A concise assessment of Springsteen at the time of the '80-'81 tour came in a quote from Bittan. "He's older and wiser, but he never strays from his basic values," the pianist said of his Boss. "He cares as much, *more*, about the losers than the winners. He's so unlike everything you

Gary Bonds sings with The E Street Band, including (l to r) Springsteen, Bonds, Garry Tallent, and Miami Steve Van Zandt and (back row) Denny Federici and Max Weinberg

think a real successful rock star would be."

Schruers recounted an anecdote he witnessed: a young fan approached Bruce at the Minneapolis-St. Paul Airport and told the singer about a friend who was seriously ill at a hospital. Later that night in concert at the St. Paul Civic Center, Bruce called the kid up to the stage and loaded him with gifts for the ill buddy. It's not something many stars would have taken the time to do, but Bruce explained, "There's not much people can count on today. Everything has been so faithless, and people have been shown such disrespect. One correct thing," said Bruce, and "then you know things can be different."

Bruce had his own ideas about what was right, and responsibility to other people topped the list. "There's too much greed, too much carelessness. I don't believe that was ever the idea of capitalism," he told Schruers. "It's just gotta be voices heard from all places, that's my main concern." Of the American dream, he noted, "It ain't about two cars in the garage. It's about people living and working together without steppin' on each other."

What *didn't* matter much to Bruce were the celebrity aspects of stardom. However, as he told Schruers, there is a benefit he accrues that is far greater than that—an intimacy, an access to secrets, that he has with the fans who

feel his music most deeply. He remembered one twenty-one-year-old who saw him and declared it to be "the most important thing in my life."

Bruce's prize was the kid's openness. "In ten minutes I'll know more about him than his mother and father do, and maybe his best friend. All the things it usually takes for two people to know each other just go away." The kid will tell Bruce his most important thoughts, and Bruce will know "that somewhere you did *something* that meant something to them. It's just a real raw, emotional thing, it's like the cleanest thing you ever felt."

That reaction says an awful lot about the kind of human

131

being Bruce is. *Musician* magazine verified our impressions of Bruce's character when it had graphologist Karl Schaffenberger analyze the handwriting of Springsteen and a few other rock stars. He found Bruce's scribblings to be "unpretentious, and very meat-and-potatoes." He conjectured that Springsteen would "soak up emotional experience like a sponge," and detected "a heavy desire for the spotlight" and "dependency on public recognition and acceptance."

The River demonstrated Bruce's popularity by zooming to the top of charts. In rock-and-roll trading circles, Springsteen paraphernalia were always popular. Bootlegs of his concerts, some said to be of stunning quality, continued to proliferate, although CBS has taken legal action to halt such bootlegging. On the legit side, a promotional picture disk of *Darkness on the Edge of Town* was coveted, as were advance copies of *Born to Run*, which were brown-tinted rather than black-and-white, and featured lettering by Ralph Steadman.

Bruce's benificence began extending not just to his audiences but to other performers. He has done more than pay homage to his predecessors by actually helping to resuscitate their careers. One of the strongest influences one hears in Springsteen's upbeat rock is Gary "U.S." Bonds, and the old Bonds hit "A Quarter to Three" was a frequent Springsteen encore. Thanks at least in part to the attention paid to him by Bruce, Bonds returned almost to the height he'd enjoyed in the early '60s.

Bruce helped produce a new Bonds album, *Dedication*, which spawned a massive hit, "This Little Girl Is Mine," and included a Springsteen-Bonds duet, "Jole Blon." And Bonds was all over the airways in a Miller Beer ad.

Mitch Ryder, the Detroit hero of "Devil with a Blue Dress" fame, hasn't come back as far as Bonds. Nevertheless, he has enjoyed higher visibility, played in more important venues on his recent tours and may be the next '60s star to enjoy a major resurgence. If it happens, it will largely be due to the tributes Bruce has paid him.

Bruce surprised many rock fans by appearing on a 1980 album by a very contemporary star, Britain's Graham Parker. The standout track on Parker's *The Up Escalator* is "The Endless Night," performed by Parker and The Rumour in a restless, indefatigable style reminiscent of Springsteen and the E Street band. So why not have Springsteen sing on the track.

It was arranged; Parker's producer Jimmy Iovine had worked on "Darkness on the Edge of Town." The teaming of Parker and Springsteen was a great vocal matchup. It's Parker's song, and Bruce never overwhelms him; he just adds an extra layer of angst to the Englishman's desire to "turn on the endless night." This is no star turn by Bruce; deferentially, he shows that he can be a valuable supporting player. Vocally, he was relating to Graham Parker as Steve Van Zandtoften relates to him.

Being an E Streeter is a busy job, but other band members did find time for extracurricular activities. Roy Bittan did

much to augment his reputation as a gifted pianist with his work on David Bowie's *Scary Monsters* and even more significantly on *Making Movies*, the finest album by Mark Knopfler and Dire Straits.

Knopfler the guitarist ventures into intricate, daring realms, but Bittan proved equal to the task of staying with him. The addition of piano made Dire Straits more solid in its rocking moments and more poignant in the delicate ones. Occasionally Bittan enjoys co-leader status with Knopfler; at other times he is showcased in instances of exquisite fragility. *Making Movies* greatly enhanced his already considerable reputation.

Bruce's career alternates between feverish public and just as feverish private activity. When the 1980-1981 tour ended, he again disappeared from sight for an extended period, but it wasn't an idle time. He was working on the songs that would eventually become album number six, 1982's *Nebraska*. It came as a surprise to just about everyone in the recording industry—undoubtedly, even to members of the E Street Band, whose work on these songs never made it to vinyl.

It's almost impossible to overstate what a gamble *Nebraska* was. The rock-and-roll audience was poised for whatever product Bruce would deliver; a long-awaited Springsteen album was a guaranteed chartbuster.

So here comes the pure heart of rock and roll with an acoustic folk album, something along the lines of Woody Guthrie or early Bob

Dylan, but even more musically spare and darker in mood. The folk idiom had thrived in the '60s, but it had virtually disappeared from the major labels and radio airplay. The household names of folkdom—the ones that were still with us—relied on loyal fringe audiences for whatever success they had. The only significant new performers who could at all be called "folkies" were the Roches, the McGarrigles, and Steve Forbert, but even their successes were modest. Forbert, rather consciously in the Guthrie-Dylan mold, had seemed like the next big thing in the late '70s, but his big moment of late was as a delivery boy in a Cyndi Lauper video.

What this all meant was that no one was waiting around for an acoustic album, not from Bruce Springsteen or anybody else. But Bruce was undaunted. He'd prepared these songs and realized they worked best with him *alone.* He took the chance.

Bruce makes news even before he makes news; rumors of his activities predate those activities by months. As Christopher Connelly observed in *Rolling Stone,* the new record was "the most surprising and talked-about record of the year—even before its release."

The program director of Cleveland's highly regarded WMMS-FM was John Gorman, who told Connelly, "There's almost nothing to compare it to." Of the response to early airplay, Gorman observed, "I couldn't believe how split down the middle the opinions were: it was exactly fifty-fifty. The audience either loved it or hated

it. There was no in-between or compromise whatsoever."

The E Street Band recorded versions of the *Nebraska* compositions at The Power Station in Manhattan, but as Columbia A&R representative Peter Philbin told Connelly, "They're songs about people gone wrong, and I think to dress up the songs with arrangements would almost have taken away from what the lyrics were saying."

Other experts seemed divided regarding the level of airplay *Nebraska* would receive, but thought Springsteen's stature would help get some exposure. Philbin believed word of mouth would of course help, although the album "in no way, shape or form is the norm in 1982." He added, however, that Bruce felt the need to make a particular statement and didn't really care about sales.

To do an album of the nature of *Nebraska,* Bruce had done some homework. In 1981 he'd performed Guthrie's "This Land Is Your Land" in concert, and he was known to have read Joe Klein's *Woody Guthrie: A Life.*

Other reading and research would shape the subject matter of *Nebraska.* Ninette Beaver, an Omaha woman who'd written *Caril,* a book about mass killer Charles Starkweather's girlfriend Caril Fugate, got a phone call from Bruce, who talked with her for about thirty minutes.

She told Bruce, "Honest to God, I know I should know who you are, but I'm just drawing a blank." Yet she recalled, "He was just a *doll* about it, really cute."

The *Nebraska* cover, shot by David Kennedy, shows an overcast sky, an endless stretch of road on a prairie seen through the windshield of a car. The inside sleeve has Kennedy's glimpse of Bruce, seen through the doorway in a chamber of one of those sturdy, middle-class, many-roomed houses they don't build anymore.

Nebraska was recorded in New Jersey by Mike Batlin on a TEAC four-track cassette recorder and mastered later by Dennis King. On the inner sleeve, Bruce once again gives thanks to Chuck Plotkin and to "Jon and Steve" (Landau and Van Zandt). The singing and the instrumentation—all of the music on *Nebraska*—are a one-man effort by Bruce.

The album begins with the elegiac harmonica and rudimentary guitar which serve as the underpinning of the title track. The narrative here was inspired by the midwest mass murderer Starkweather, a story which in turn formed the basis of the film *Badlands* starring Martin Sheen and Sissy Spacek. As in most Springsteen songs, the first line creates a visual image that pulls us right into its midst. The protagonist first saw his girl twirling her baton, which is how Sheen first spies Spacek in the movie.

"Nebraska" is a chiller because Springsteen, writing in the first person as the killer not actually named, captures the banality that made the real-life Starkweather and the screen Sheen so frightening. This murderer is no "mad dog" and he doesn't seem demonic; "thrills" don't enter into his actions either. His

133

emotional range is remarkably curtailed; one gets the impression he killed people to see if he'd register any feeling at all. He speaks of "fun" and "meanness" but we sense very little of that. "Nebraska" is an acute portrait of a man so numb he is capable of evils a feeling man might not bear.

"Atlantic City" is a glimpse of that shore community during its metamorphosis into a casino resort. These moments are pivotal for the fate of the town but also for the character whose role Bruce sings. There's an opacity to what he tells us, but it's intriguing to possess only a few of the details. This bloke has been down on his luck, struggling to survive, and is only one step ahead of people who might be described as lethal. What's touching is the nature of his optimism: he tries convincing himself that a love that's cold and even dead can be rekindled. On "Atlantic City," Springsteen's vocal is doubletracked, with the harmony part high and distant, and consequently desperate and haunting. A mandolin (or maybe just the high end of the guitar) adds poignancy to the hero's plea for enduring romance.

"Mansion on the Hill" was inspired by drives Bruce took with his father to a solitary house outside of his New Jersey hometown. Each line etches another detail in the landscape; we know the roads and the fields nearby, the lights and the music and the children at play along the route. Since it has such basic instrumentation and is sung so quietly, it might seem like a sad song, but it's only sad in the way that any reminis-

cence is wistfully tinged with remorse. This song could have been done with the same lyrics in a more upbeat fashion, but then it wouldn't belong on *Nebraska*.

"Johnny 99" is the first track on the record that can be called rock and roll. It's very much in the '50s style; the chords and strumming (acoustic, not electrified) could belong to Elvis or any of a half-dozen other idols of the era. It's the first *Nebraska* track not sung in the first person and the first that deals with the travails and frustrations of the working man.

The protagonist is an auto worker, who loses his job, can't find another, gets drunk and ends up shooting a man. His sentence is prison for "98 and a year." Given a chance to speak, "Johnny 99" tells of the hardships that drove him wrong: the bank was about to take his house. His despondency is so deep that he tells the judge to change his sentence and execute him.

The outstanding composition on *Nebraska*, and as riveting a 5:39 vignette as anyone's written in years, is "Highway Patrolman." Some films would take two hours to accomplish what Springsteen does in a few minutes; you can listen and ask yourself which actors should play Joe Roberts, Franky, and Maria.

"Highway Patrolman" is one more variation of the Cain and Abel story. One brother's good and the other's bad, but these two don't hate each other. Joe, the patrolman, has "always done an honest job." Of his brother Joe, who is laconically eloquent, can only repeatedly say, "Franky ain't so good."

For all his life, Joe has been

bailing Franky out of trouble Joe's two strongest characteristics are his basic decency and his filial allegiance, yet Franky's behavior always puts those two principles in conflict.

There is much that Joe and Franky share; they laugh and drink and dance with Maria, whom Joe marries when Franky goes into the army. Joe's dictum is that blood runs stronger than anything, and that a man who doesn't stand by his family isn't much of a man.

Ultimately, Franky will commit the crime that can't be ignored, and it is Joe's duty to bring him to justice. Naturally, the question becomes, "Will he or won't he?" As the brothers' two cars follow each other in the Midwestern night, you don't know, and you sure wonder.

Quite simply, this is one of the greatest stories Bruce has ever told. These are very real people, there is genuine tension, and the conflicts Joe Roberts feels are very clear to us. And remember, the deck isn't so totally stacked against Frank's virtue. Although his misdeeds are chronicled in detail, it is he who went into the army while Joe got a farm exemption and married Maria. The question of what one owes and to whom has never been treated as brilliantly in song as it is on "Highway Patrolman."

Based on an endlessly recurring, chugging, four-note guitar riff, "State Trooper" is stark even in the context of this bare-bones album. The setting, a rainy night on the Jersey Turnpike lit by the refinery's fires, could be on any Springsteen album. Here, however, the driver may be

Bruce Springsteen with bassist Garry Tallent in background

the most desperate and pained character on *Nebraska*. "State Trooper" shares with "Atlantic City" a "less is more" approach to lyric writing. From Bruce's urgent singing and his final howl, we sense that life is a nightmare for this narrator, but we only have a few clues to put together as to the nature of these horrors. He speaks of his "baby" but also asks that his prayers be heard; he imagines the trooper's happy lot in contrast to his own disappointments. Thanks to Bruce's performance, we feel the depth and nature of the man's torment even if we ain't clear about its cause. But Bruce isn't cheating us; it's more effective this way. This fellow's anguish is so general he's not likely to communicate specifically its causes to us.

Side two's opener, "Used Cars," is another soft and somber piece of music, but the mood is one of anger and determination. Springsteen gives us picturesque details of his family members sitting in the latest of a line of used cars his father will buy. To the hero this is an indignity, and he swears if he wins the lottery his used-car days will end. These, fans of Bruce know, are themes drawn from his own life; the lyric about the father who toils so long in a monotonous job echoes Bruce's frequent comments about how hardworking *and* disappointed his own father was. Like many of the *Nebraska* tracks, this one is about a man who hasn't gotten his share of society's pie and swears that that will change. The difference is that the details could have come directly from Bruce's life; he's not writing about someone else.

"Open All Night" reflects another side of the automotive experience. This and "Johnny 99" are the record's only real rockers, and Bruce sounds like a late-'50s guitar hero as he gives an account of a night-shift worker whose only wish is to get him and his car to his girlfriend Wanda's place. Anyone who's driven in the "wee wee hours' sun" can relate to the images of "Open All Night," when vision may be hallucination, gas stations are the lone outposts of civilization, and religious programming clogs the radio dial. The E Street Band is absent of course, but 135 with its detailed descriptions of auto parts and turnpike landmarks, this song definitely puts us on familiar Springsteen turf.

"Open All Night" turns out to be the upbeat track between "Used Cars" and the next number, "My Father's House." This is one of the record's more cryptic tunes, a recounting of a ghostly dream with Bruce as a child, frightened and perhaps lost in the wilderness as he may be chased by the devil. Finally, he spies his dad's house and collapses into his arms.

The adult Bruce awakens from the dream, contemplating the difficulties between him and his father, and goes to the house to make amends with his father, only to be told by a stranger that he doesn't live there anymore.

Like "Highway Patrolman," "My Father's House" is a highly cinematic vignette, each line representing a scene. The ending may be seen by Christians as religious allegory, with "My Father's House" representing the Church. However, given the frequency with which Bruce's troubled relationship with his father has been part of his recorded oeuvre, the song can also be seen as a sigh about the difficulty of bridging the gap between father and son.

"Reason to Believe," with Bruce on harmonica and guitar, ends the album, and it's the bluesiest number on *Nebraska*. Here is a tale of a search for purpose and meaning, of the need to find sense and order in what can seem an arbitrary world. In each verse Bruce recounts a separate scene—a man's fixation with a dead dog, a

woman waiting for the lover who deserted her to return, a baptism, and a funeral—and observes that whatever may happen, people find some way to have faith in something.

Springsteen approaches the final verse more quietly and slowly—with stealth and caution, in fact. A man and a large congregation wait for a wedding ceremony down by the riverside, but the bride never appears. The man can only watch the river flow and wonder where she is—but Bruce again reminds us that at day's end "people find some reason to believe." This is an ode to perseverance; no matter what occurs, we must keep on keeping on.

The *Nebraska* arrangements are spartan, more bare than anything from Dylan or Forbert, and that starkness is often the source of the fear the tracks generate.

On paper, these songs *read* like they're Springsteen's, but the mood and the sound are certainly a change of pace. One has to be amazed by a guy who can change horses like this and still come out shining. Yet perhaps it shouldn't surprise us too much. The man who did "The River," "Independence Day," and "Meeting Across the River" can sparkle in this kind of musical setting.

We're impressed by how very American *Nebraska* feels. Bruce is quintessentially of the U.S.A., like Gary Cooper or Sam Shepard. This isn't the America of the sloganeers or phony patriots but the land of soil and blood and sweat. Springsteen gets to the gristle and the marrow of Americanism, far beneath surface slogans. His isn't

empty "we're so great" posturing. It's a real examinatio. of just what and who we are The chic band of the week doesn't delve into that. A fev figures like John Cougar Mellencamp and Michael Stanley may work in this vein, but they aren't Bruce. His songs have a ring of authenticity found nowhere else in rock. And he is less of a poseur than any other major rock performer.

In his *Rolling Stone* review, Steve Pond theorized that *Nebraska* was "flying in the face of a sagging record industry with an intensely personal project that could easily alienate radio." With a bold stroke, Pond believed, Bruce had reclaimed "his right to make the records *he* wants to make, and damn th consequences."

Pond saw the album as a "violent, acid-etched portrait of a wounded America that fuels its machinery by consuming its people's dreams." There was great care in its seeming simplicity; it was "ar acoustic triumph" within which "every touch speaks volumes."

For Pond, *Nebraska* was "as deep and unsettling as anything Springsteen has recorded." It might also be "his narrowest and most single-minded work," one which adopted established styles, but Pond felt that helped create the record's "clear, sharp focus."

Time magazine reviewer Jay Cocks considered *Nebraska* in tandem with Billy Joel's 1982 release *The Nylon Curtain* and proclaimed, "they are about the process of contemporary craziness, and they are devastating." Cocks saluted Springsteen for such a "serious, ambitious" record at a time when the rickety structure of the business was resulting in music of "bantamweight escapism."

Cocks noted that *Nebraska* sounds "a little like a Library of Congress field recording made out behind some shutdown auto plant." The themes and scenes might have appeared before in Springsteen's work, but the nuggets Bruce mined from this milieu were innumerable. "He can get the same sort of mythic resonance from this setting that John Ford took out of Monument Valley," Cocks observed.

One publication where rock record reviews aren't usually found is *The Christian Century,* but the magazine saw much to ponder in *Nebraska.* In "Springsteen's richest and most textured lyrics to date,"

the magazine observed, a "celebration of street life has become a howl of protest, alienation has turned to desperation, and the questions Springsteen raises have taken on a new and frightening urgency." It predicted "the busiest critics will be the Marxists, for the album fairly overflows with images of class struggle."

The reviewer thought *Nebraska* was replete with "strangers and sojourners struggling through the dark side of life, guilty heroes who must make nighttime pilgrimages to the sea to 'wash these sins off our hands.' Humankind's need of grace is the overarching theme." The themes embraced by Springsteen—questions of evil, sin, the baring of illusions, human values and priorities, obligation and responsibility, pride

and shame—were enough for this Christian periodical to take notice of *Nebraska,* an album in which "no one is spared the burden to accountability, and none of us can free ourselves or the world from the mire of sin."

In the kind of interpretation one won't find in *Downbeat, The Christian Century* suggested that the father in "My Father's House" could indeed be *The* Father, and that the story of the groom waiting for his bride in "Reason to Believe" could be a variant of a New Testament tale of Christ as a groom and the Church as his "imperfect bride."

The idea that Bruce should be treated as a serious literary figure was given credence by University of California (Santa Barbara) Professor Frank McConnell, writing in a 1983 issue of

Bruce with the Big Man, saxophonist Clarence Clemons

Commonweal. To McConnell, Springsteen is "a legitimate American mythologist, a storyteller of clear and authentic talent and, I would say, a major American poet."

The professor compares Bruce to F. Scott Fitzgerald, observing that both men explored the myth of success as opposed to the actual price success extracts. To McConnell, Springsteen was also restating an insight of Reinhold Niebuhr, understanding that "the essential irony of American history was its inability to distinguish between expectation and the inevitable disappointment of expectation: we hope for everything, forgetting that that hope itself is self-defeating." Finally, like Henry James, Bruce considered the impossibility "that to be *truly* wealthy was to be able to satisfy every requirement of the imagination."

Not all notices were so glowing. The division of opinion about *Nebraska* is best illustrated by the comments in *Stereo Review* by Steve Simels. Simels was a fan, believing Bruce was "the one mainstream rock star who maintains a genuine give-and-take relationship with his audience." And Simels believed that the evidence of Bruce's storytelling strength was here. "As vignettes they're wonderful," he said of the compositions. "'Highway Patrolman' is going to make a heck of a movie someday."

As entertainment and music, on the other hand, *Nebraska* severely disappointed Simels. "It sounds like it was written for rock critics, rather than people," he wrote, calling most of the album "well, *boring.*" Simels felt Bruce had

said far more about blue-collar plight and been more fun when he contributed the song "Out of Work" to Gary Bonds' *Dedication.* On *Nebraska,* Simels found that "tunes are less than minimalist, the tempos are uniformly dirgelike" and there persisted an "overpowering miasma of fatalism and gloom." He saw Springsteen as a victim of the artist's "compulsion to make the Big Statement every time out."

On the down side, *Melody Maker* said *Nebraska* offered "tired, weary, old observations that tell us nothing we don't already know," and *Boston Rock* felt it was "only for those who like to ponder the hopelessness of everything while drinking themselves into a long stupor."

Frankly, the negative criticisms of *Nebraska* are somewhat mystifying. The quiet beauty, the soulfulness, and the dramatic impact of the album are undeniable. It's not a party record and it's not for every mood. Yet one doesn't criticize Bill Murray for not being Laurence Olivier or Sting for not being Placido Domingo. *Nebraska* isn't a supercharged rock-and-roll album, but it is remarkably and uniformly effective in its own way, which is *very much* its own way. On the terms dictated by Bruce, I don't see how *Nebraska* can be considered anything less than a monumental recording. Those who fail to perceive the worth of songs like "Highway Patrolman" can't really be listening.

Ultimately, the consensus of critics was generally favorable. The 1982 *Village Voice* Pazz & Jop poll, which sur-

veys a wide array of national critics, had *Nebraska* tabbed as the third best album of the national critics, behind only Elvis Costello's *Imperial Bedroom* and Richard and Linda Thompson's *Shoot Out the Lights.*

Bruce was also where he had been two years earlier—at the top of several categories in the *Rolling Stone* Reader's Poll. He won Artist of the Year honors and was voted top male vocalist and best songwriter. *Nebraska* was picked as album of the year.

While *Nebraska* was becoming a solo project, other E Street Band members had their own musical undertakings to pursue. 1982 saw Miami Steve Van Zandt's first album incarnation as Little Steven and the Disciples of Soul on *Men Without Women,* the first vehicle for Steve's songs since he'd written for Southside Johnny. On Christmas Eve of the same year, Van Zandt was married, with Bruce as best man. The ceremony was performed by the one and only Little Richard.

Clarence came up with an album, too. Recorded with his band, The Red Bank Rockers, in 1983, *Rescue* featured two tunes by Bruce. And the video of the Big Man's single, "A Woman's Got the Power," included the first video incarnation of Bruce, who appears for a few seconds at the end as a car wash attendant.

Meanwhile, Bruce was making his presence felt in the recordings of other artists. After he got together with Warren Zevon, "Janey Needs a Shooter," one of Springsteen's many unrecorded songs, radically changed and was retitled "Jeannie Needs a

Shooter." It turned up on Zevon's *Bad Luck Streak in Dancing School* and on the live *Stand in the Fire*. A concert video of Zevon also includes his rendition of Bruce's "Cadillac Ranch."

Despite his immense popularity, Bruce hadn't been played on black-orientated stations. He made a small entry into that market when his song "Protection" was recorded by Donna Summer in 1983, and he backed her on guitar. And Bruce hadn't made it onto the country charts, but Johnny Cash did record two songs from *Nebraska*, "Johnny 99" and "Highway Patrolman."

Springsteen's material began emerging in unlikely places. The manic comedian Robin Williams did a routine in which Elmer Fudd bids for rock stardom by testing his creaky voice on Bruce's "Fire." The quiet, seething menace of the song was severely undermined by Mr. Fudd's inability to enunciate consonants, especially R's.

A witty tribute to Bruce came from the frequently caustic Randy Newman on his 1983 album *Trouble in Paradise*. The record's funniest song— maybe the most bitingly hilarious thing Newman or any other singer has come up with in years—is "My Life Is Good." A teacher's criticism of his son causes the proud Newman to boast of his wondrous accomplishments and impressive connections, one of which is with a "Mr. Bruce Springsteen." As Newman sings it, Bruce told him "Rand, I'm tired/How would you like to be the Boss for awhile?" Well, of course, it's his triumphant moment. As he instructs his "Big Man" to

blow (it's Ernie Watts, not Clarence), the exultant Newman can claim that his life is indeed good.

A weird adjunct to the Springsteen phenomenon also came between *Nebraska* and the release of Bruce's seventh record. It was a film called *Eddie and the Cruisers,* the story of a leather-jacketed '60s bandleader. Although the whole film abounds in anachronisms, Eddie resembles no one as much as he does Bruce Springsteen. This is partly because the soundtrack was created by the Rhode Island bar band John Cafferty and Beaver Brown, folks whom Bruce has gigged with and who had already been observed as having a sound similar to Springsteen's. Much of the filming was done in Asbury Park, and Eddie's musical sidekick was a black saxophonist. The film's technical adviser was Southside Johnny, who had pointed out several inaccuracies in an early script. Director Martin Davidson says he saw Eddie as a blend of Dion, Jim Morrison, and Springsteen, but the sound and feel is chiefly Springsteen a decade too soon. Most people saw *Eddie* as a shameless rip-off; actually, most people didn't see it at all.

That changed in 1984 when the film played on several cable stations, causing a ground swell of interest in the soundtrack, which became a bestseller after having done limited business upon its initial release. The unexpected windfall caused Cafferty and Beaver Brown to hold back a newly recorded album as they belatedly raked in the

chips from *Eddie.*

The coupling of rock music and motion pictures was becoming more prevalent than ever before. It was only one of many major changes in the music business over the past several years—changes that made integrity an even tougher commodity to stick by.

In an era of glitz, when style counts for more than substance and virtually everyone has made concessions in search of glamour, Springsteen remained enormously faithful to his own vision. He was not interested in the show biz trappings. He was dedicated to the music and the performance, not to the attendant hype.

MTV and the whole music video explosion were in full swing before any response from Bruce was forthcoming. With a few very creative and entertaining exceptions, the videos were boring, meaningless, self-indulgent and even insulting. There was a great deal of speculation as to how the uncompromising purist Springsteen would respond to this new adjunct to the music business.

Thus far, he has thoroughly resisted the temptation to make any "dramatic" videos or to engage in huge production numbers which could not illustrate his compositions any better than the pure performance could. The first task at hand in the face of the video explosion was to come up with something from *Nebraska*. The ingenious solution was a teaming of the song "Atlantic City" with documentary black-and-white footage of the seaside town, particularly its conversion into a gambling resort. It conveyed exactly what Bruce wanted to say about Atlantic City, and he didn't have to act in it.

By 1984 a few tapes of Bruce in concert, though several years old, were made available to music video programs; a high-voltage "Rosalita" became the most popular of these. The release of "Dancing in the Dark" as the first single from a forthcoming 1984 album forced Bruce again to face the video question. This time he would appear in his own promo spot. It would be a first experience for him and for the director who was selected—Brian DePalma.

DePalma might have seemed a strange choice. Although noted for dazzling visual imagery in general, his work is known in particular for its artful gore. His films *Carrie, Dressed to Kill, Blow Out, The Fury,* and most recently *Body Double* are frequently bathed in blood.

DePalma left his exploding crimson pellets at home. His teaming with Springsteen was a masterstroke—no frills, just Bruce at his best, exultant in performance. A battery of cameras caught the new muscular Bruce on stage, singing with a grin that would make the American Dental Association proud and swaying his hips in time to the E Street beat. Most of the principal photography was done at the tour opening in St. Paul, although additional footage needed to be taken later on. The video is rather straightforward. If there's plot at all, it's the eye contact and growing attraction between Bruce and an extremely pretty, fresh-faced young woman he spots in the first

row. By the end of the video, he's pulled her onstage and they are "Dancing in the Dark" together.

In the 1980s the "straight" press was paying more attention to rock, and Springsteen's latest peak of popularity (with the release of "Dancing in the Dark") did not escape their eyes and ears. Liz Smith, who usually pays mind to the likes of Liz Taylor and Jackie O, devoted a long televised gossip segment to Springsteen, focusing on his reclusiveness, his reluctance to do interviews, videos, or act in any way like a star. Declaring him to be the Garbo of rock, Smith found Bruce's lack of flamboyance extremely refreshing.

Springsteen finally did grant a national TV interview during the 1984 tour he'd do behind his 1984 album, *Born in the U.S.A.* It was given to, of all people, Barbara Howar of "Entertainment Tonight." Charming but perhaps embarrassed, smiling even though his mouth was always half closed, Bruce was the epitome of politeness. The biggest news that came out of the session was Bruce's explanation of how he plans what will please his fans. There are no intricately contrived calculations, as he explained. He just tries to do what he finds entertaining, and figures it will work for the audience. What a simple formula!

The ultimate accolade from the establishment press may have come on September 3, 1984, when Springsteen made the cover of *People.* He's in a black leather jacket, flashing a pearly smile, next to type that heralds a "rare

interview" with a man the mag openly claims has "the best rock 'n' roll show on the road."

The cover and inside shots are by David Gahr. The interview is by Chet Flippo, who considers Bruce the "poet of the blue-collar baby boomers" and *Born in the U.S.A.* to be "a blue-collar anthem of the '80s."

As is by now known in rock legend, the genesis of *Born in the U.S.A.* came in the long drives Bruce took around the country. Woody Guthrie may have traveled by a different route as a railroad hobo, but he and Bruce were both astute observers of the landscapes both of nature and of faces. They shared a concern for the ordinary folk, along with an understanding that there is nothing *ordinary* about them.

"I've always enjoyed traveling like that," Bruce told *Rolling Stone*'s Debby Miller about his car trips with a friend. "It was always kinda liberating for me. I was only recognized twice. You get out there, and people don't really care that much about two guys just driving."

Born in the U.S.A. addresses itself to the people who haven't had reason to notice that good times are supposedly upon us. Bruce himself has referred to it as "survival music."

It has that sound. The percussion on the title track is ingeniously appropriate to the working milieu; the cowbells, cymbals, and whatever else all sound like someone is punching a time clock or ringing the 5 P.M. bell. The backbeat of "Working on the Highway" is the rhythm of hard manual labor.

Within 48 hours of its June 4 release, *Born in the U.S.A.* was a platinum album. By the end of July, it had attained double platinum status. The album, recorded at the Power Station and The Hit Factory, was produced by Springsteen, Landau, Van Zandt, and Chuck Plotkin. The cover, with photography by Annie Leibowitz, is a rear view of Bruce, in T-shirt and jeans against the stripes of our flag.

It takes almost no time to realize that *Born in the U.S.A.* is an exceptional record. The freshness it injected into a moribund radio repertoire made it Bruce's most significant contribution to rock music in nine years.

Bruce and the E Street Band produce a sound that is sharper, more solid, and more richly textured than ever before. The opening sounds of *Born in the U.S.A.* are absolutely anthemic. It's a monumental moment; Max's forceful drumbeat and the metallic keyboards on the title track give the impression that an entirely new "U.S.A." is being forged on the anvil of rock and roll.

In the time he takes between records, Springsteen travels, searches, and matures. He meets Americans and comes to understand their needs and predicaments. The title song encapsulates many of the concerns he's made his own. There is a dichotomous approach to patriotism on this album. It comes decorated in the colors of the flag, but *Born in the U.S.A.* is largely a cry of anger and frustration with the state of America.

For many Americans below the upper-middle class and under the age of 45, *Born in the U.S.A.* is a pretty fair summation of the facts in 1984. The hero of the title track was born in a backsliding town and never had anything easy. First comes trouble, then Vietnam, then joblessness and difficulty with his V.A. benefits. He may be a "cool rocking Daddy in the U.S.A.," but as he sits on the outskirts of town there is no map showing his future. In 4:39, this captures the status quo as well as any tune released during the year.

"Cover Me" became the second single off the album, although it only managed to reach about number eight. It continues the theme of rough times, but the narrator here is more overwhelmed. He can't articulate the particulars, but does convey the enormity of his plight. He wants a woman who will stand between him and the world, a world he is so hesitant to face that it appears he'd rather not go out the door. "Cover Me" isn't one of the standout tracks on *Born in the U.S.A.*, but it does feature some nicely raunchy guitar and a powerful, thumping bass.

The playing on this album is *determined* and *athletic*. Mighty Max is at his mightiest, the guitars are most primal, and the keyboards add whatever color, fills, or support each song requires. "Darlington County" benefits from all of these; its feel is muscular *and* joyous, as if the guys were celebrating the fact they're at their physical peak. The situation is in some ways still the same as in the earlier tracks. These are young, blue-collar types looking for jobs, but the feeling here is more positive. The singer and his buddy Wayne

are coming into the county of the title (we don't know what *state* it's in) expecting employment from Wayne's uncle and a good time from the local girls. Theirs seems to be a charmed road existence: these are big-city studs from New York with some money to spend and good times on their minds. They figure the locals are pushovers and there are no limits to what they can do. Fortunes, alas, do change. As the odyssey continues, Wayne disappears. And as he leaves "Darlington County," the hero spies his friend handcuffed to a police car.

"Working on the Highway" is centered around a simple Eddie Cochranish guitar riff and loads of handclaps; rhythmically, it compares to "Summertime Blues." This is a terrific track. Listen closely to a Springsteen song and observe what becomes apparent time and again; there may not be anyone who sets entire stories to music as well as he does.

Maybe Bruce will spin a white-collar yarn one day, but this isn't it. It's a workman's saga, with evocative lyrics and more than a bit of irony. At the close of their work week, men go separate ways, some with wilder plans than others. Our protagonist is a young man building a new highway who's entranced by an even younger girl he runs off with against her father's wishes. They get along fine, but her brothers pursue this little miss—who is under legal age. The hero goes to jail and to a work detail where, once again, he's "working on the highway."

At a slower tempo, "Downbound Train" comes next with **141** its acoustic guitar and organ arrangement and its striking scheme of rhyming couplets. For my money, this is far and away the best track on *Born in the U.S.A.* and one of the strongest tunes Bruce has ever recorded. It may not be as readily digestible as some songs receiving more airplay, but programmers were wrong not to feature this track, and CBS may have erred in not pushing it.

As other writers have indicated, sequencing matters so much on Bruce's albums. "Downbound Train" really fits in right after "Darlington County" and "Working on the Highway" and just in front of "I'm on Fire." In the first couple of lines, we learn the hero had a solid, happy life. The rosy picture changes (they tend to on this record) and the job is gone and so is the girl, who achingly announces her departure. The "rider on a downbound train" motif is a way of explaining our man's negative progress.

To say that a great deal of thought goes into the recording of Bruce's records is an understatement. He's assembled one of the finest musical aggregations extant, but sometimes the most appropriate thing for them to do is not do very much at all. The dramatic shift in this song comes when virtually the entire band drops out and only Federici's eery organ remains. When Bruce mentions hearing a voice, it might be a dream. What follows is a verse at first hopeful, then heartbreaking. As the hero pursues what he's visualized, Federici's organ gives him a step-by-step accompaniment. These two alone are devastating; this middle section is one of the most unnerving passages Bruce has ever come up with. Few songs of this caliber came out of anyone in 1984.

"I'm on Fire" is another increment softer. To put it bluntly, the singer here is randy with desire. His woman is now keeping company elsewhere, and he openly asks if her lover "can do to you the things that I do." How does this kind of lone-

Springsteen takes bows with (l to r) Clarence Clemons, Max Weinberg, Nils Lofgren, Patti Sciafa, Roy Bittan, and Danny Federici during 1984 *Born in the U.S.A.* tour

liness feel? Bruce describes it in wrenching detail, and it's a pain involving every sense he has. We get the picture. The track ends with Bruce howling, not loudly but very desperately. It's a brief song, but its meaning comes through.

"No Surrender," the pounding rocker that opens side two, is most notable for having the line which pretty much sums up the motivations of Bruce and his E Street colleagues: "We learned more from a three-minute record than we ever learned in school." It's performed at a blistering tempo chiefly established by the Mighty Max. Once again, the characters are people who've grown up together and known each other for years.

"No Surrender" is perhaps more cryptic than the other songs here. The friends' vow not to "surrender" appears to be a promise never to grow stale with age, to remain passionate and vital and tuned into the life of the street. Yet maturity comes, and it doesn't seem so hard to wear. The singer's buddy observes the "war" in the streets and figures it's not theirs to fight anymore. And the singer is contented and comfortable just to be quiet and asleep with his lover in the country. Sounds like every adult's greatest desire.

A sort of "wall of sound" accompanies "Bobby Jean," a somewhat melancholy reminiscence about a longtime friend who quite suddenly disappears from home without saying goodbye. One prominent deejay guessed that Bobby Jean was male, figuring that these lyrics could not pertain to a female.

It's true that there's no solid indication of romance here, but it's also true that the kind of platonic camaraderie described could exist between a man and a woman in this modern era. Right? In any case, the last line refers to Bobby Jean as "baby."

Bruce expresses regret that there was no last goodbye, even though he knows whatever motivated Bobby Jean's departure wasn't anything he could have solved. Still, these were great, proud buddies who had the same tastes and shared so much even when other folks shunned them. This is a major loss: Bobby Jean understood him like no one ever did or will again.

It's possible Springsteen is actually calling out to a real friend he has lost track of; he wishes that somewhere out there this friend will hear what he's singing. Bruce has again touched a universal chord; surely every one of his listeners has wistful remembrances of at least one friend of whom he's lost track. Spirits are lifted a bit at the end of this track as Clarence and his sax get a chance to soar.

If side one focuses chiefly on the struggles of the worker (which do, of course, affect personal lives), side two is more concerned with private matters. The singer of "I'm Goin' Down," another old-time rocker, is getting nothing but aggravation from the woman of his dreams. His kisses, which once sent her into ecstasy, are now received tentatively. The entire experience just drives him "down."

The carefree innocent days are over; Springsteen was almost thirty-five when he made this record, and not all things come so easy anymore. Illusions drop away; confronting reality can be painful, and what was satisfying yesterday won't suffice today. "Glory Days," like "Bobby Jean," is a celebration of old friendships, but there's a difference. Bruce's alliance with Bobby Jean extended into the present, whereas "Glory Days" talks about the guys who dwell on past exploits. This is another Gary Bondish track (there's a 60's rock-and-roll organ, not a modern synthesizer) in which Max and Danny are most prominent.

The personalities in "Glory Days" are the former baseball star who sits in bars remembering what a pitcher he was, and the beauty who stopped everyone in their tracks; she's now a divorced mother who recalls those days to keep herself from crying. The singer hopes he'll avoid the pitfalls of looking back, but ultimately realizes that as time passes, the glorious tales of youth are what remain. These are not the comments of a young man who sees unlimited promise ahead of him; this man's been burned and disappointed.

If "Downbound Train" is the best composition on *Born in the U.S.A.*, "Dancing in the Dark" must be the most superlative performance. It's a crackling, absolutely perfectly constructed track, with every element precisely in place, beginning with the French horn synthesizer alarum and the terrific Tallent and Weinberg foundation. Bruce's singing is magnificent. In a rock song, his phrasing, emphasis, and modulation have

143

probably never been more on target. And the balance is terrific; if you're not listening closely, you may not even hear jangling rhythm guitar, but it supplies much of the propulsion. For 4:01 no one lets up, not even Clarence, who, after a record full of gut-busting sax playing, gets a chance for a nimbler, smoother solo as the track trickles out.

The facility that Bruce displays as a songwriter is astounding. The rhyme scheme of "Downbound Train" was close to *aabb;* "Dancing in the Dark" is more *abab,* but there is nothing contrived about these structures. They fit as comfortably as a glove.

The singer of "Dancing in the Dark" doesn't have an easy life. His routine leaves him exhausted and empty. He'd like to chuck it all.

Unlike some of the other tales of restlessness on *Born in the U.S.A.,* this one contains hope. This guy's not beaten; he knows somewhere life can be better. He reaches out to a girl who's got her own inertia to overcome. Transcending their shoddy circumstances is a cooperative venture to Bruce, and he declares his availability. How great to come near the end of this record and hear from a fellow who won't be beaten, and who in a gesture recognizing personal need but somehow seeming generous, can reach out and suggest that he and she climb out of their morass together. There isn't a thing about "Dancing in the Dark" you'd want to change. It thoroughly deserved its chart-topping position.

After side two's batch of songs, "My Hometown" has to come as a surprise. Although we might not have expected a song like this, it soon seems that Bruce once again made the right choice. This becomes a perfect denouement, as if "Dancing in the Dark" were the height of excitement and "My Hometown" a hazy nightcap.

The surprise is that this is just so exquisitely beautiful. The other astonishing thing is, well, you always think you know how good Bruce is and then he comes up with a pearl like this. The important themes of *Born in the U.S.A.* are etched in our minds. But Bruce has something left, a painfully moving tale of life and hard times in "My Hometown." It could be Asbury Park (a lot of the details apply) but it could be told by any guy in his mid-30s living in an industrial town. Bruce is aided vocally on "My Hometown" by Ruth Jackson.

Anyone who's followed Bruce for over a decade can recognize these hometown vignettes, especially the poignant opening image. The eight-year-old sits in a Buick with his father—that father who loved to drive—and tells his son, with pride, we assume, to look out and see "this is your hometown." The first chorus, and all the others, repeat the "hometown" line three more times, long enough for the listener to conjure up a mental picture of his or her *own* hometown.

This tale moves across the years, the years passed through by anyone of Bruce's age. The mid-'60s racial tensions he sings of were part of Asbury Park and many northern cities in those years. The details of the third chorus—a vacated Main Street, a loss of population, the closing of the mills and reduced employment—are all a part of urban America today.

Still, these are people's hometowns, and they want to stay, they want to feel community, a sense of shared pride, a belonging. In the last stanza, the singer and his wife (he's now 35) think about leaving for a more fertile clime. But, in the last line, this new father is telling his own son "this is your hometown." This full-circle approach was part of "Working on the Highway," but that was more ironic. This is real; it happens everywhere. A man grows up in the town his father grew up in, and his son will do the same. The feeling of having a place, since the earliest days, is what America has always been about. Often, however, it's a promise that has turned empty or bittersweet. That's why "My Hometown" is the perfect closer to *Born in the U.S.A.*

The E Street outfit is democratic. Clarence and Roy Bittan had stood out on recent albums, but on *Born in the U.S.A.* we begin to notice Gary Tallent more, and the spotlight quite often shines on Federici and Weinberg. Max truly merits kudos here; he gives a sturdy, consistent performance on this record.

Born in the U.S.A. is the record everyone needed in 1984. With meaningless ephemera so dominant in contemporary music, an album of such substantial content, masterful performance, and crisp production is a virtual rescue mission for rock and roll.

And, for whatever reasons, lots of Americans needed to be reminded that while we're all glad to be here, not everyone is on a smooth ride in this U.S.A. Portions of Springsteen's audience are as old as he is, and they know that the time comes for cataloging and understanding setbacks, and rekindling the urge (as in "Dancing in the Dark") to proceed anew. Younger fans might just be starting to face the real world, with less insulation or protection, the perils of an uncertain economy, and relationships that can't be fairy tales anymore. Finally, the album served notice to the few remaining doubters that Bruce as a performer and songwriter is still vital, fresh, and pioneering. He hasn't forsaken his dream or his talent.

In *Newsweek*, Jim Miller found "new songs of rare simplicity and depth" on the latest album. He conjectured that while Springsteen had previously "strained to give his songs a rhythmic stature by writing about romantic stereotypes," he was now displaying "a welcome air of restraint." To Miller, "Dancing in the Dark" was "sunny and spacious. He called the falsetto ending of "I'm on Fire" "one of the purest, most affecting moments on record this year."

In the *Village Voice*, Robert Christgau noted the care with which Bruce toils in the studio. "Springsteen and Landau are crazed perfectionists, shuffling songs and risking techno-hubris not in pursuit of the hook or the beat but of sound and vision that evolve so slowly they appear to progressives not to change at all." Change had taken place, however, as Christgau noted. "His music really has evolved enormously, so that

the records which gained him national recognition now seem relatively murky and overblown even to those who didn't mind those flaws at the time."

Of the new effort, the *Voice* pundit commented, "We shouldn't underestimate the role of studio perfectionism in the ringing live intensity of *Born in the U.S.A.*'s sound, but on songwriting and singing alone it's an amazing feat. Not since *London Calling* has any album brought rock and roll's traditional affirm-in-the-negative to such a

pitch of consciousness, and Bruce's outreach exceeds the Clash's by a factor of 10."

Born in the U.S.A. is a supremely solid, masterfully rendered effort. It may be unfair and unrealistic to expect something as groundbreaking as *Born to Run* was in its day; that only happens two or three times in a decade. We're used to Bruce now, and it's not to be expected that something from him will sound as exotic and remarkably different as *Greetings* or *Born to Run* did to folks who first heard them. Neverthe-

less, his new work is a stretch. He extends and expands his musical craft and his lyrical messages. The sound of *Born in the U.S.A.* is sharper than on any other Springsteen recording. His singing is more assured than ever, and his songwriting is gaining strength at a rate we can feel comfortable with. In an age of effluvia, *Born in the U.S.A.* seems revolutionary if only because it is so heartfelt and substantial.

As a bonus for Springsteen fans, "Dancing in the Dark" was made available in a dance remix by Arthur Baker. It was an engaging version that got airplay for awhile but soon gave way as the original moved to the top of the charts, battling it out with Prince's "When Doves Cry." A similar mix was done on "Cover Me," featuring echo treatments of the original vocal.

The flip side of the "Cover Me" single was a rarity, a Springsteen recording that was live and was not his own composition. It was recorded at the New Jersey Meadowlands on July 9, 1981, and was a song that fit Springsteen like a glove—Tom Waits' "Jersey Girl." By way of introduction, Bruce tells the crowd, "I wanna thank you guys for making this feel like home for us."

Right before Christmas in 1984, the third single would be "Born in the U.S.A." itself, and a 12-inch dance version was released at the same time. The accompanying video again consisted of performance clips, this time intermingled with positive and negative images of life in these United States. At the end, Bruce stands facing the flag with his back to us, just as on the album cover. But in the last moment he glances over his shoulder, just to let us know that it was indeed

Bruce with saxophonist Clarence Clemons

his flip side we'd been admiring.

On the new 45, Bruce put a song on the flip side that hadn't appeared elsewhere on vinyl. It was getting to be a habit. Before the unreleased "Jersey Girl" had backed "Cover Me," the B side of "Dancing in the Dark" had been the popular "Pink Cadillac."

The newest B side was the ominous "Shut out the Light," a chiller that caused "Time" reviewer Jay Cocks to write, "This single song is under four minutes long but packs a punch stronger than most albums." It's a primarily acoustic track, featuring guitar and fiddle with a closing harmonica solo. The subject is again a working-class young man trying to make adjustments; "Shut out the Light" could have fit in nicely on either *Nebraska* or *Born in the U.S.A.*

Although it's not plainly stated, we can surmise from certain details and from our familiarity with Bruce's concerns that the man landing on the airport runway in the opening line has just returned from military duty, almost certainly in Vietnam. His homecoming is joyous for everyone else; his wife makes sure they'll be alone and she'll be her loveliest, and Pa is sure he'll get his factory job back. The hero, however, is haunted. He lies awake at 4 A.M., unable to move his hands, and cries in the repeating chorus "I got the shakes and I'm gonna be sick." At the end, he's alone in a Maryland forest, staring into the dark waters of a river. Rather than look at a potentially brighter future, he "dreams of where he's been."

By 1984, most of us realized that coming home wasn't simply a matter of setting foot on U.S. soil. Here, Springsteen articulates the problem succinctly in 3:45.

People who'd experienced rough times had Bruce's empathy, and by the time *Born in the U.S.A.* was released, he could state in an interview with Chet Flippo, "Mainly all my records try to offer some sort of survival course. Maybe you can't dream the same dreams when you're 34 that you did when you were 24, you know, but you can still dream something. Maybe you've got to downsize some of your expectations. I know I have. Just in growing up, in accepting adulthood. My characters, I think that's what they do. They say, 'Man, I had some ___ ___ ___ ___ thrown at me, but here I still am.'"

The strength of the middle class impressed Bruce in the form of his sister Virginia and her husband and two children, a family that had started very young and made it through shaky going. "My sister's tremendously, unbelievably strong," Springsteen told Flippo in *People.* "This is real inspiration. Like in the song 'My Hometown,' these are the heroic things that happen in most people's lives. Everyday things between them and their kids."

There is a marked change in Bruce's more recent songs, and it may explain why he elects not to do so much of the early material in concert. The consistent thread is the extreme vividness of his characters. The early ones might have cartoonish, mythic identities, but the new ones could be the guy in the

apartment downstairs or the family next door. Or *you.* Maybe that's what it is. He isn't singing about somebody *else* we might recognize. He's singing about all of us.

That's why his audiences don't have the blue-collar homogeneity some critics would suggest. The crowd can also include preppy Ivy Leaguers and Wall Street types who've come to consider rock totally ephemeral but see Bruce as the one substantial exception.

Robert Christgau noted, ". . . perhaps 40 percent of the crowd at Byrne [the 1984 New Jersey Meadowlands shows] was female, which is abnormally high for hard rock, with lots of women-together couples, which is almost unheard of. The age spread of 15 years or so was also abnormally high."

Before Bruce embarked on that 1984 tour, some personnel changes had to be made. Van Zandt, as Little Steven, was ready with a second album. The separate venture was encouraged by Bruce, who felt Steve was too important a creative force not to be on his own. Steve himself told *People* writer Lisa Russell, "I felt that my time with Bruce was very worthwhile, but that I'd gone as far as I could go with that collaboration." He added, "I felt he still wanted and needed me. But it's time to move on."

The replacement as E Street guitarist was Nils Lofgren. Still in his early thirties, Nils was from the Washington area and had guested on a Crazy Horse album and played a key role in Neil Young's *After the Goldrush* at the age of seventeen. In his teens he had a band called Grin, which recorded the memorable *1 + 1* including a perfect piece of light, infectious pop, the track "White Lies." Nils did more work with Young and recorded a string of solo albums for A&M. His most famous composition may be "Keith Don't Go," a tribute to Keith Richards for giving "the message to millions."

Lofgren's solo work was always interesting (it featured collaborations with Lou Reed) but he never became a superstar and despite a critically acclaimed *Wonderland* album in 1983, he had been dropped by MCA, his most recent label. He played a bar-band tour and an acoustic tour with brother Tom before he was asked to replace Van Zandt.

Nils has the same kind of raw fervor and energy as Springsteen and has always given the impression of loving nothing as much as making music. His addition to Bruce's lineup seemed logical and appropriate. Years before either was well known, Bruce and Nils had both auditioned at the old Fillmore West on the same night. Their rapport was instantaneous, and it remained solid whenever they crossed paths on the rock-and-roll road.

The other addition to the concert lineup was Patti Sciafa, formerly a singer with Southside Johnny. Reportedly, Bruce had heard her singing Motownish material in an Asbury Park club. She was apparently the only person Bruce knew who could hit all of his material's high notes. One male New York deejay marvelled that she "has the longest legs I've ever seen." Speculation suggested that she and Bruce were in-volved offstage as well as on.

The *Born in the U.S.A.* tour was preceded by a surprise show a few weeks earlier at New Jersey's Stone Pony. The tour itself opened in St. Paul, and there were no problems selling tickets. Ten shows at the New Jersey Meadowlands grossed $3,232,000. In the first hour of sale, they were going at a rate of 280 per minute, almost double the previous Teletron/Ticketron record. The tickets were gone in a day.

Except for Michael Jackson, who would draw a very different audience at cavernous arenas for higher-priced tickets, there probably isn't a musician alive who could draw such a mammoth response. It was evidence that despite his long absence from the concert scene, the legend of Bruce as an unparalleled live attraction remained strong.

The 1978 edition of *Current Biography* described Springsteen as "a slightly tightly muscled young man invariably described as 'elfin.'" Frankly, that may be the only place he was *ever* called elfin. In any case, those folks should see the new athletic and powerful '80s Springsteen.

The 1984 Bruce was someone anybody's parents could respect. There are no drugs, no tobacco, and very little alcohol in his life, and his health consciousness has seen him chisel his body into a taut form reminiscent of Marlon Brando in *A Streetcar Named Desire.* For the extreme demands of the concert tour he was undertaking, Bruce seemed to be in great shape.

The concerts are physically trying workouts, both for the fans and for Bruce. More than one observer commented that Springsteen frequently uses massive doses of Ben-Gay. Bruce, who told Flippo he'd never exercised before in his life, lifted weights and ran six miles daily under the supervision of trainer Phil Dunphy. At the age of 34, only a supremely conditioned athlete could go through what Bruce does in concert.

There's no prepackaged quality to Springsteen's shows. They're rehearsed, and the band is beautifully tight, but things differ each night. When WNEW-FM's Dave Herman noted that Max Weinberg's eyes followed Bruce wherever he went on stage, Max admitted that it had to be that way. The segments were well-prepared, but it was not often obvious what Bruce would do next.

If he isn't singing or playing, if the music is in the hands of the other E Streeters, he's always doing something to build crowd enthusiasm. As seen in the "Dancing in the Dark" video, he's become a dancer at ease. He was heard to say during one 1984 show, "I ain't shy anymore."

There are spectacles one sees at Springsteen's concerts that won't be glimpsed at any other rock show. Bill Barol in *Newsweek* commented, ". . . in a touching, if weird, moment, the overwhelmingly teen-age audience at the Byrne Arena rose to give Mr. and Mrs. Springsteen a standing ovation. There isn't another performer in rock and roll who could inspire such heartfelt devotion." There's enough fan affection for Bruce to extend to his parents and probably even distant relatives.

The order and song selection changes in these three-to four-hour shows, and even "Twist and Shout" may show up. A frequent opener, however, is an anthemic "Born in the U.S.A." It's a stirring beginning. "It's unbelievable," said one photographer who'd seen it more than once. "It's monumental in rock and roll."

Except for "Rosalita," it's rare to hear much of anything from the first two albums in concert now. Almost everything from *Born in the U.S.A.* is there, of course, but one of the pleasant surprises is how well the *Nebraska* material has been adapted for live shows.

After three or four energetic openers, it might be time to bring in this less ferocious but still emotionally powerful music. Lofgren duets with Bruce on guitar for "Atlantic City," and Bruce and Patti sing together on "Mansion on a Hill."

On that song, Bruce tells of drives with his father to a big white house outside of town. "It became very mystical, like a touchstone," he told the St. Paul crowd. "And now when I dream, I'm sometimes outside the gate looking in . . . and sometimes I'm the man inside."

That's a personal experience, but Bruce has more universal ones he can share with his audience as well. Before doing "Used Cars," he explained, "if you've ever pushed a car down the street and felt like the biggest jerk in the world, this one's for you."

The tour featured an encore that might have surprised some fans. It was the fifteen-year-old "Street Fighting Man" by the Rolling Stones. Bruce had a simple explana-tion for why he included the song. It wasn't the political content he was interested in. Quite simply, he'd always wanted to sing the lines, "What can a poor boy do / 'cept to sing in a rock-and-roll band?"

Jim Sullivan, reviewing the Worcester show for the *Boston Globe*, declared, ". . . no rock 'n' roll artist puts across a concert with more verve, depth, and emotional intensity." He witnessed "a stirring performance that felt honest, righteous, and wholly satisfying." Sullivan made it clear that Bruce's cockiness is not arrogance but actually a joyous form of democracy. When he boasts, said the writer, "he boasts for everyone." Furthermore, he understands that he's an embodiment of everyone's fantasy. "I'm real lucky," Springsteen said at the Worcester Centrum. "I get to live a little bit of my dream every night."

When it comes to gauging rock stars, Bruce Springsteen is "somewhere off the high end of rock's Richter scale," opined Bill Barol in *Newsweek*. To Barol, Bruce is "the most generous of rock-and-roll performers" and "puts on the biggest-hearted show in pop."

Barol saluted Springsteen's newfound dance mastery, observing, "His repertoire extends from the twist to a stately rumba with sax-ophonist Clarence Clemons, even to an attempted moon-walk à la Michael Jackson."

Barol theorized that the strength of Springsteen's new album came from an inherent tension in which "despair and defiance slug it out in every line." Fortunately, defiance is usually victorious, and "hope never dies."

One man who'd seen it all in rock and roll and thought Bruce was the genuine article was Chris Chappel, Bruce's assistant road manager after a long affiliation with The Who. Chappel first saw Bruce at London's Hammersmith Odeon in 1975, and as he told Chet Flippo, "I knew immediately that the rock 'n' roll torch had been passed from the Beatles and the Stones and The Who to him. I had never seen such a great show. And I still haven't."

To Flippo himself, the rest of the performers deserve praise. He believed "the E Street Band is solid enough to support the World Trade Center."

Springsteen's stature and renown far exceed the usual parameters of the rock world, and straighter elements have taken note of him. Who better personifies that realm than the conservative columnist George Will, who was invited to a Springsteen show by Max Weinberg's wife Rebecca?

Will, who said Bruce "resembles Robert DeNiro in the combat scenes of *The Deerhunter*," was a bit condescending in his comments on the rock milieu and made trite insinuations about the aural overload of the concert (he listened with cotton in his ears). And he said that the vaunted "values" Bruce sings about are often "cars and girls."

Nevertheless, he was impressed by the intensity and effort Bruce and his colleagues put out. "An evening with Springsteen," he wrote, "is vivid proof that the work ethic is alive and well." The band was a bargain, and the fans were more than pleased. "How many American businesses can say that?" Will asked. Protectionism—guarantees of fair markets for domestically produced goods—would be unnecessary, he concluded, if all Americans "made their products with as much energy and confidence as Springsteen and his merry band make music." With so much "lackadaisical effort" and "slipshod products" abounding, Will felt anyone who performs "conspicuously well and with zest is a national asset."

To Bruce, being back in touch with his people seemed to mean the most. "The contact with the people who come down to see us has been the most sustaining thing through the years," he stated in *USA Today*. "You sustain that relationship by being responsible about it." To Bruce, that meant what the paper's writers Bruce Pollock and Anne Ayers called "the longest, most intimate, most spontaneous and most carefully crafted show on the road." And to Bruce, there was nothing he'd rather give. "I'm out there doing something at night that I can never get from anything else. I guess I feel most at home onstage."

The give-and-take with the audience is unique. In the final analysis, what can be said about Bruce is that he treats people like they're people. He's not standoffish or superior. He doesn't insulate himself with publicists and other flacks. He is an egalitarian, and his fans love him for it.

His creative stage raps are intimate revelations between friends. In an evangelical mode, he'll say, "Do you believe that if you die during the course of this show, due to the excitement, that you're going to heaven?" And later, in an intro to one of his best-loved rockers, he'll declare, "God created the Pink Cadillac, and He said it was great!"

The stories help forge that special relationship Bruce has with his audiences. As Flippo observed, "he becomes a beneficent uncle, and the crowd is transformed into rapt children, hanging on every word."

Springsteen told Flippo what it means to be onstage before his faithful. "Some nights when I'm up there, I feel like the king of the world. It's the greatest feeling on earth. I can go home and get in bed and sleep real sound. It's a beautiful thing. Beautiful. It can tune you into everything, what's happening with people everywhere."

It's something hundreds of thousands of fans wanted to share. In some cases, they might have to pay dearly. For shows in Los Angeles, scalpers were reportedly getting as much as $425 a seat.

Bruce had no control over that, but he did make contributions beyond his very generous concert performances. During the midst of the 1984 tour, it was announced that Springsteen had donated $10,000 to a food bank set up by a United Steelworkers local in Pennsylvania.

There's a lot of diversion required to fill the long hours on road journeys, especially

on as lengthy a tour as Springsteen was undertaking. Entertainment is required, and he helps supply it. Apparently he is a big "Honeymooners" fan, and in improvised bits he often plays Ed Norton to the Ralph Kramden of road manager Bob Chirmside.

There are even the occasional nights off and, between gigs in Hartford and Philadelphia, Clarence Clemons squeezed in an appearance on "Late Night" with David Letterman. Introduced as the man who more than anyone else "helped restore the saxophone to the prominent place it once held in rock and roll," Clarence performed a Dave Edmunds tune with Paul Shaffer's crackerjack band, playing in the mold of "Yakety Sax" man Boots Randolph.

Clarence was an engaging talk-show guest, discussing his minor-league football career, revealing that his own Red Bank Rockers would be touring without him as Johnny and the Rockers, and referring to his Selmer tenor sax as "my other woman." He revealed that while the best sax reeds are made in Cuba, our diplomatic standoff with that country means he gets his from France. Talking of his dual life as an E Streeter and a Red Bank Rocker, Clarence praised his own luck and said it was like "having your cake and eating it, too."

The rascally Letterman, on a later show, included a joke about Springsteen in a quiz show parody. The viewers were asked to identify which of four elements was not a recurring theme in Springsteen's songs. The choices

were driving on the old highway, driving with girls, driving in New Jersey, and sushi. Pretty funny.

With more rock performers making film debuts, and with Bruce's songs becoming more cinematic all the time, there is always speculation about his making movies himself. In an interview with Debby Miller of *Rolling Stone* he explained, "when I write the song, I write it to be the movie—not to *make* a movie, to *be* a movie." The songs are a few minutes long, but as he says, "you could really screw it up in an hour and a half."

The songs are complete, they stand on their own, they give a listener everything he or she could want. Nothing is left out. They tell whole stories—the incidents, the crises, the emotions at hand. Within a couple of lines, you are in a place, and soon enough you are living with real human beings.

This is why Springsteen does not need to make music videos and does not need to become a movie star. He's correct in believing in his music as fervently as he does. Attempts to further adorn it will only diminish it.

He is a master of rock-and-roll craftsmanship. No one asked Pablo Picasso to write a novel. No one asked Tolstoy if he could sculpt in bronze. Why ask Bruce Springsteen to *act* or make movies?

The scope of Bruce's popularity was evinced when the progressive New York station WNEW-FM asked its listeners to name their three favorite songs of all time. "Stairway to Heaven" by Led Zeppelin took the top spot, but in second was "Born to Run," often

proclaimed as the unofficial anthem of New Jersey.

At number 13 was "Thunder Road," with "Jungleland" at 16, indicating *Born to Run* had had the most lasting impact of Bruce's albums. "Rosalita" was at 27 and "Dancing in the Dark," the single at the time of the voting, came in at 56. "Backstreets" was number 123, "New York City Serenade" surprisingly high at 171, "She's the One" was 181, "Spirit in the Night" was 199, and "Badlands" was 225. The first track from *The River* was "The Ties That Bind" at 273. In the rest of the list of 1027 songs, only two cuts from *Born to Run* were missing, but nothing from *Nebraska* was picked, not even "Atlantic City."

By the time he set out on the *Born in the U.S.A.* tour, some recent large changes had taken place in Springsteen's life. He now lives in a three-story brick manse in the upscale town of Rumson, New Jersey. It has a swimming pool and an extremely long driveway. Fans, mainly female, drive vast distances for the chance to glimpse Bruce, or leave him a handwritten note. The local police are on guard, making sure no one is too intrusive.

And the star of enormous magnitude still makes very little of his status. "Rock star" is a tag that makes Bruce laugh. "That's Like 'Celebrity Bowling' or 'Hollywood Squares,'" he told Michael Muston in *Us Magazine*. "I always wanted to be a rocker, a rock 'n' roller."

"The trappings and stuff are a joke," he continued. "The only fun of sitting in a lim-

ousine was if you weren't supposed to be in it." To Bruce, "the hype just gets in the way. . . . All the stuff you dream is there, but it gets diluted by all the other stuff that jumped on you by surprise."

Just having that house was a far cry from the early days, when he had no fixed address. He talked of that period in *USA Today*, remembering, "it was like, you live in this apartment and then you run out of money and you go to this guy's house and for a while." At the time of *Greetings*, he stayed on a friend's floor and recalls, "I used to enjoy the feeling of not having a place."

His sentiments about his parents changed, too. By 1984, son and father and mother were getting along fine. The teen years had been hard, but he surmised, "finally, you realize your dad is just a guy, your mom is just a girl. They've got their own ideas, and their own dreams."

In his mid-thirties, other attitudes were taking new shape. "I love kids. I love women," he told *USA Today*'s Pollock and Ayers. Music and fellow musicians were centerpieces of his life for so long, but he declared, "I think you can have everything. I don't think I can't because of my business." Still, he felt no sense of urgency. "It comes around when it comes around," he concluded.

Cars remained a passion. Bruce has a good-sized flotilla in his Rumson garage, but his everyday fave was a ten-year-old Ford pickup. "It's all beat up," he said. "If you hit something it doesn't matter, as long as it's inanimate. I've smashed into several things with it, coming home late at night."

There was continuity in his life; in some ways, that's what sets him apart. Robert Christgau noted that Bruce "identified so strongly with the guys he grew up with that he swore he'd never forget them. Many rock and rollers have contracted amnesia behind such vows," said Christgau, while Bruce "still hangs out on the Jersey shore, living a distinctly 'normal' life for a star of his magnitude. All he wants is a chance to speak to and for every one of his own." Throughout his career, even amidst the prolonged legal agonies, that is the one right and honor Bruce has striven to maintain.

By 1984, Bruce's influence was felt in many sectors, but another distinction was added; he became an issue in a presidential campaign. President Reagan, speaking in New Jersey, tried scoring points with the locals by saying how much he admired the hopefulness in the songs of their native son, the Boss. Walter Mondale retorted that Reagan was tarnishing one of New Jersey's heroes, and said Bruce "may be born to run but he wasn't born yesterday." Mondale suggested that Reagan misunderstood the full message of Bruce's work and speculated that the Democrats would earn Mr. Springsteen's support. When pressed, White House representatives couldn't name Mr. Reagan's favorite Springsteen tunes. Bruce remained mum through this strange episode, but he was reportedly displeased that Reagan was quoting his lyrics.

As 1984 drew to a close and speculation about 1988 began, perhaps supporters might consider drafting Springsteen himself for president. He was now old enough for the job, and Clarence Clemons would make a terrific Secretary of Defense.

It's a thought. However, *Born in the U.S.A.*, both the album and the tour, give us a greater inkling of how Bruce Springsteen will be spending the remainder of the 1980s. He is a more perceptive and literate songwriter than ever, and he is learning more about the art of record production with each new release. He is a more generous concert performer, crafting long and exciting shows which illustrate the wide range of his musical knowledge and ability.

He is an observer of contemporary America, and his focus seems sharper and broader at the same time. The wisdom he gathers filters down to his audience in songs which say so much so acutely in such a small amount of time. Unlike almost any major rock star, he communicates compassion, sympathy, and universality. Yet lest all of this seem far too weighty, he never forgets that rock and roll is celebration, and he and the E Street Band remain the finest onstage partyers in the music business.

In this decade, it often seems that expanding the borders of the rock-and-roll art form means finding new dimensions in outrageous superficiality. For Springsteen, growth clearly means much more. Few artists continue to progress and be important after ten years at the top of the heap. For Springsteen, however, every new step is a major breakthrough. There's ample reason why his records and concert tours are the most eagerly anticipated in all of music. And his grasp of that distinction isn't likely to change soon.

153

DISCOGRAPHY

SINGLES

BORN TO RUN/MEETING ACROSS THE RIVER
CBS 3661
Released October 1975

TENTH AVENUE FREEZE OUT/SHE'S THE ONE
CBS 3940
Released February 1976

PROVE IT ALL NIGHT/FACTORY
CBS 6424
Released June 1978

BADLANDS/SOMETHING IN THE STREET
CBS 6532
Released July 1978

PROMISED LAND/STREETS OF FIRE
CBS 6720
Released October 1978

BORN TO RUN/MEETING ACROSS THE RIVER
(re-issue)
CBS 3661
Released February 1979

HUNGRY HEART/HELD UP WITHOUT A GUN
CBS 9309
Released October 1980

SHERRY DARLING/BE TRUE
CBS 9568
Released February 1981

THE RIVER/INDEPENDENCE DAY
CBS A1179
Released April 1981

THE RIVER/INDEPENDENCE DAY/ROSALITA
(Come Out Tonight)
12" CBS A13 1179
Released May 1981

CADILLAC RANCH/WRECK ON THE HIGHWAY
CBS 1557
Released August 1981

ATLANTIC CITY/MANSION ON THE HILL
CBS A2794
Released October 1982

OPEN ALL NIGHT/THE BIG PAYBACK
CBS A2969
Released November 1982

DANCING IN THE DARK/PINK CADILLAC
CBS A4436
Released May 1984

DANCING IN THE DARK (extended remix)/
PINK CADILLAC
12" CBS TA4436
Released May 1984

DANCING IN THE DARK/PINK CADILLAC
(picture disc)
CBS WA4436
Released May 1984

COVER ME/JERSERY GIRL
CBS A4662
Released August 1984

COVER ME/JERSEY GIRL/DANCING IN THE
DARK (dub version)
12" CBS TA4662
Released August 1984

COVER ME/JERSEY GIRL (picture disc)
CBS 4662
Released October 1984

COVER ME (undercover mix)/COVER ME (dub
mix)/SHUT OUT THE LIGHT/DANCING IN THE
DARK (dub mix)/JERSEY GIRL
12" QTA 4662
Released March 1985

ALBUMS

GREETINGS FROM ASBURY PARK, NEW JERSEY
CBS 65480.
Released 1973.
Re-issued November 1982 as CBS 32210.

Blinded By The Light/Growin' Up/Mary Queen Of
Arkansas/Does This Bus Stop At 82nd Street/Lost
In The Flood/The Angel/For You/Spirit In The
Night/It's Hard To Be A Saint In New York City.

Personnel: Bruce Springsteen (guitar/vocals),
Clarence Clemons (sax), Garry Tallent (bass), Vini
'Mad Dog' Lopez
(drums), David
Sancious (piano),
Danny Federici
(organ).

Produced by Mike
Appel and Jim
Cretecos.

THE WILD, THE INNOCENT, AND THE E STREET
SHUFFLE
CBS 65780.
Released 1974.
Re-issued November 1983 as CBS 32363.

The E Street Shuffle/4th Of July, Asbury Park
(Sandy)/Kitty's Back/Wild Billy's Circus Story/
Incident on 57th Street/Rosalita (Come Out
Tonight)/New York City Serenade.

Personnel: Bruce
Springsteen (guitar/
vocals), Clarence
Clemons (sax), Garry
Tallent (bass), Vini
'Mad Dog' Lopez
(drums), David
Sancious (piano,),
Danny Federici
(organ).

Produced by Mike
Appel and Jim
Cretecos.

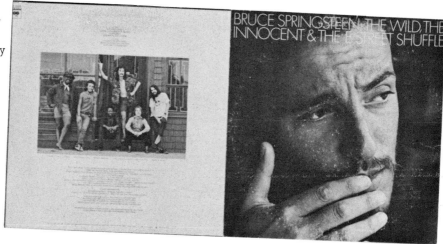

ALBUMS

BORN TO RUN
CBS 69170.
Released October 1975.

Thunder Road/Tenth Avenue Freeze-Out/Night/
Backstreets/Born To Run/She's The One/Meeting
Across The River/Jungleland.

Personnel: Bruce Springsteen (guitar/vocals),
Clarence Clemons (sax), Garry Tallent (bass),
Danny Federici (organ), Max Weinberg (drums),
Roy Bittan (piano).

Produced by
Bruce Springsteen,
Mike Appel and
Jon Landau.

DARKNESS ON THE EDGE OF TOWN
CBS 86061.
Released May 1978.

Badlands/Adam Raised A Cain/Something In The
Night/Candy's Room/Racing In The Street/The
Promised Land/Factory/Streets Of Fire/Prove It All
Night/Darkness On the Edge Of Town.

Personnel: Bruce Springsteen (guitar/vocals),
Clarence Clemons (sax), Garry Tallent (bass),
Danny Federici
(organ), Max
Weinberg (drums),
Roy Bitten (piano),
'Miami' Steve Van
Zandt (guitar).

Produced by
Bruce Springsteen
and Jon Landau.

ALBUMS

THE RIVER
CBS 88510.
Released October 1980.

The Ties That Bind/Sherry Darling/Jackson Cage/
Two Hearts/Independence Day/Hungry Heart/Out
In The Street/Crush On You/You Can Look (But You
Better Not Touch)/I Wanna Marry You/The River/
Point Blank/Cadillac Ranch/I'm A Rocker/Fade
Away/Stolen Car/Ramrod/The Price You Pay/
Drive All Night/Wreck On The Highway.

Personnel: Bruce
Springsteen (guitar/
vocals), Danny Federici
(organ), Max Weinberg
(drums), Clarence
Clemons (sax), Garry
Tallent (bass), Roy
Bitten (piano), 'Miami'
Steve Van Zandt
(guitar).

Produced by Bruce
Springsteen, Jon
Landau and
Steve Van Zandt.

NEBRASKA
CBS 25100.
Released September 1982.

Nebraska/Atlantic City/Mansion On The Hill/
Johnny 99/Highway Patrolman/State Trooper/Used
Cars/Open All Night/My Father's House/ Reason
To Believe.

Personnel: Bruce Springsteen (guitar/vocals).

Produced by Bruce Springsteen.

ALBUMS

BORN IN THE USA
CBS 86304.
Released June 1984.

Born In The USA/Cover Me/Darlington County/
Working On The Highway/Downbound Train/I'm
On Fire/No Surrender/Bobby Jean/I'm Going
Down/Glory Days/Dancing In The Dark/
My Hometown.

Personnel: Bruce Springsteen (guitar/vocals),
Clarence Clemons (sax), Garry Tallent (bass),
Danny Federici (organ), Max Weinberg (drums),
Roy Bitten (piano), Steve Van Zandt (guitar).

Produced by
Bruce
Springsteen,
Jon Landau,
Chuck Plotkin
and Steve Van
Zandt.

From his meager beginnings in central New Jersey to the successes of "Born to Run," "The River," and "Born in the U.S.A.," here's Bruce at his most driven and his music at its most passionate and powerful!

Two of the biggest events in the rock world recently were the release of Springsteen's much-talked-about album "Born in the U.S.A." and the launching of his year-long international tour. The album quickly reached the number one spot on the charts, selling one million copies within forty-eight hours of its release and earning Bruce another platinum record. Two singles from it—"Dancing in the Dark" and the title track, "Born in the U.S.A."—also surged to the top in sales. The tour has played to sellout crowds all across the country.

Few rock and roll artists continue to progress and prevail after ten years at the top of the heap, but Springsteen is one who does. For him, every new step is a major breakthrough. There are lots of reasons his records and concerts are the most eagerly awaited in all of contemporary music. Unlike almost any other rock star, he communicates compassion, sympathy, and universality. Yet he also never forgets that rock and roll is celebration, and he remains the finest onstage reveler in the business.

In *Bruce Springsteen*, Peter Gambaccini shows that Springsteen is every bit as marvelous and gifted as his most zealous fans believe him to be. No star performer invests so much of himself in his music and in his performances. For a public personality who is also a man of the people, there can be no greater tribute than the passionate reception given Springsteen's concerts and albums.

Cover photograph © by Ebet Roberts

ISBN 0-7119-0696-3

ISBN 0.7119.0696.3
Order No. OP 43397

9 780711 906969

90000

Omnibus Press